A

MW01222839

a version of Ibsen's PEER GYNT
*set in the Pacific Northwest
and points south,
drawn freehand and writ large*

Eric Overmyer

BROADWAY PLAY PUBLISHING INC
56 E 81st St., NY NY 10028-0202
212 772-8334 fax: 212 772-8358
http://www.BroadwayPlayPubl.com

ALKI
© Copyright 1997 by Eric Overmyer

First printing: June 1997
ISBN: 0-88145-126-6

Book design: Marie Donovan
Word processing: Microsoft Word for Windows
Typographic controls: Xerox Ventura Publisher 2.0 PE
Typeface: Palatino
Copy editing: Liam Brosnahan
Printed on recycled acid-free paper and bound in the USA.

BY ERIC OVERMYER
PUBLISHED BY
BROADWAY PLAY PUBLISHING

NATIVE SPEECH *(1984)*
ON THE VERGE *(1986)*
IN PERPETUITY THROUGHOUT
THE UNIVERSE *(1989)*
IN A PIG'S VALISE *(1989)*
MI VIDA LOCA *(1991)*
DARK RAPTURE *(1993)*
DON QUIXOTE DE LA JOLLA *(1993)*
THE HELIOTROPE BOUQUET BY SCOTT JOPLIN AND
LOUIS CHAUVIN *(1993)*
FIGARO/FIGARO *(1996)*
AMPHITRYON *(1996)*

Alki—a Salish word meaning 'by and by'. The second syllable, 'ki'—rhymes with pie.

I'd like to thank Stan Wojewodski and Rick Davis of Center Stage for first suggesting I take a whack at PEER GYNT; Jeff Steitzer of A Contemporary Theater for encouraging my notion to set my version in the Pacific Northwest; Richard Hamburger and Melissa Cooper of Dallas Theater Center for doing a reading of Part One at their Little Festival of the Unexpected; and Kip Gould of Broadway Play Publishing for publishing the revised manuscript.

This play is for Lily Xiao Xia Parmelee Overmyer

CHARACTERS
in order of appearance

PEER
HANNAH GYNT
BAD OTTER
FIRST YOUNG LADY
SECOND YOUNG LADY
SMITTY
FIRST PAL
SECOND PAL
THIRD PAL
BAKER
FIRST WOMAN
PA JOHNSON
JOHN JOHNSON
FIRST YOUNG LADY
SECOND YOUNG LADY
SALLY
MA JOHNSON
PREACHER ROWE
INGRID
FIRST FERAL GIRL
SECOND FERAL GIRL
THIRD FERAL GIRL
WOMAN IN GREEN
GIANT RACOON
KING
FIRST HAINT
SECOND HAINT
THIRD HAINT
FOURTH HAINT
FIFTH HAINT

VOICE
ALBERTA
UGLY BOY
MR COTTON
MONSIEUR DUBOIS
HERR EBERKOPF
LORD WIMBLE
SEÑOR VASQUEZ
SIGNOR TRESCA
APE
AMAZON INDIAN GIRL
AMAZON INDIAN WARRIOR
REMEDIOS
HERR DOKTOR BIELDFELDT
DR ALVAREZ
ORDERLY
CAPTAIN
FIRST MATE
MYSTERIOUS STRANGER
COOK
PETER
TUMBLEWEEDS
MR BONES

PART ONE

ACT ONE

Scene One

(The Puget Sound Territory, 1851. Tall trees. Endless forest. A cold & rocky shore. An overcast summer day. PEER, *a wiry, raggedy youth of twenty, appears, followed by his scolding mother,* HANNAH GYNT.*)*

HANNAH GYNT: Liar!

PEER: Ain't!

HANNAH GYNT: Lies, lies, more lies, and damn lies, salted over with stretchers for seasoning, and pure unadulterated whoppers for dessert.

PEER: Honest, Ma, I swear.

HANNAH GYNT: Don't swear, son. Your nose is getting longer by the minute, and your eyes is turning dark dark brown.

PEER: Every word true, so help me Jesus.

HANNAH GYNT: Now you've done it. Taking God's name. Well, go ahead. Tell it again. See if we ain't struck dead by lightning right here in broad daylight. Tell me how you been gone six long weeks, and come home empty-handed, clothes in tatters and lost your rifle, and nothing to show for your meanderings but a mouthful of outlandish foolishness, and us with no more 'n a thimbleful of dried salmonberries in the larder and winter already whispering in the wind and the wolf scratching at the door. Go ahead, tell it. See if I believe you this time.

PEER: Happened just like I said. I hiked all the way to Mount Tahoma—

HANNAH GYNT: That's more 'n ninety mile—

PEER: Took me a week of hard walking, too, and never mind the weather, nor the shoe leather, nor the mosquitos, neither. Skeeters so big they could stand flat-footed and consummate the vows of Holy Matrimony with full-grown wild turkeys. So there I was, beset on all sides by hostile elements and nature red in tooth and claw. Living on nothing but wild berries, and salmon from the streams, which I caught with my bare hands like a grizzly bear, just swooped 'em out of the water like that!

HANNAH GYNT: Goodness gracious. And I suppose you ate them salmon raw—

PEER: Don't be silly, Ma. I had my flint. Why even in a howling rainstorm, when the drops are sharp 'n hard 'n sideways like bullets, I can conjure a fire that'll make the Devil take off his shoes and warm his feet.

HANNAH GYNT: His cloven feet—

PEER: His cloven feet.

HANNAH GYNT: And then? Where'd you spy this mighty buck?

PEER: I'm getting to that. I hiked for days towards Mount Tahoma. Through forest, marsh and meadow. And I seen lots of game. Deer and badger and elk. But I let 'em go undisturbed.

HANNAH GYNT: Did you? That's kindhearted of you, and us near starving to death with not two copper pennies to rub together since your no-good wastrel father took off like a thief in the night with what was left of my daddy's money, after he'd drunk up or gambled or whored most of it away—

PEER: Ma, that was fifteen years ago—

HANNAH GYNT: And still sticks in my craw every time I think about it. So tell me again why you disdained to harvest the providential bounty all around you?

PEER: I knew what I was looking for, and weren't about to waste my powder on the paltry, puny, and pecunious.

And there in the forests of the foothills of Mount Tahoma,
I found him.

HANNAH GYNT: The buck—

PEER: The most magnificent buck you ever seen, Ma. Tall at
the shoulder as two men. Broad across as a river in spring
flood. And antlers like the King of Poland's good-time
chandelier. Must've been thirty points on that head, prob'ly
more.

HANNAH GYNT: I ain't never seen a buck that size—

PEER: Nor me neither, not 'til now. I swear, Ma, this
creature was bigger 'n Paul Bunyan's blue ox, Babe.
By half—

HANNAH GYNT: *(Drawn in)* Gracious. So you really seen
him, after all. Then what happened?

PEER: He looked at me, and I looked at him, and I swung
my rifle up and pulled the hammer back, and at the sound
he lit out for the mountaintop, leaping from ridge to ridge
faster 'n a greased pig at a Swedish roof raiser. And I let
loose with a shot that not one man in a thousand could
have made.

HANNAH GYNT: Missed him completely, I 'spect.

PEER: No, m'am. I got him, alright. Caught him on the fly
as he was taking the next ridge in a single bound. Dead
center, through the shoulder, under the rib cage, and
nicked his heart. That was some shot, if I do say so myself.
Like clipping the wings off a baby hummingbird at a
hundred yards.

HANNAH GYNT: And so he dropped like a gutshot duck,
did he?

PEER: No, m'am. That buck was so big and so strong, he
barely flinched. Just kept flying up the mountain, leaping
from rock to rock like the biggest mountain goat you ever
seen. And I'm running after him, best as I can, picking out
his trail by climbing a couple hundred feet up into the trees
every mile or so to find a broken twig or a trace of blood,
where he'd gone flying by.

HANNAH GYNT: A flying buck, if that don't beat all. Oh,
I wish I could've seen that!

PEER: Oh, he was something alright. I tracked him through
that trackless forest for three days and three nights, the
trees so big they blotted out the sun, so I couldn't tell what
time of day it was, and the weather up top completely
different from the weather on the ground, snowing one
place and raining the other, and that buck moving so fast
I didn't dare stop to eat or sleep, just lived on berries
snatched along the way, and such morning dew as I could
suck from the very air—tracked him all the way around
the base of Mount Tahoma, must've been a hundred miles,
easy, and he couldn't shake me, try as he might. So then he
started up the mountain, and by the fifth day he wasn't
flying no more, just walking, but still moving pretty strong,
straight up the mountain, across glaciers and icefields and
old lava flows and fields of vertical scree, and there wasn't
nary a handhold or a place for a person to put his feet, and
many's the time I thought I was gonna lose my grip and
fall a thousand feet straight down and end up dead and
lonesome on some godforsaken pile of broken rock—

HANNAH GYNT: But you didn't, thank heavens—

PEER: No, m'am. I didn't. I kept my footing, and I kept my
resolve, and I tracked that buck up hill and over dale and
all the way to the top of Mount Tahoma. And there I stood
at the very apex of the world, smack dab in the middle of
the Good Lord's bountiful Creation, and I could see all the
way to Canada one direction, and all the way to California
the other, and I could see the great Pacific Ocean shining in
the distance, and China on the horizon—

HANNAH GYNT: China! My word! Was it upside down?

PEER: Not the part I could make out. Looked plumb
right-side up to me. And I could see the Columbia and the
Snake rolling down to the sea all silvery, and where Paul
Bunyan and Babe the Blue Ox carved out Puget Sound and
made the Cascades with what dirt and stone was left over
from their mighty excavation—

HANNAH GYNT: And what about the buck, son? What
about the poor buck? Mortally wounded and failing fast—

PEER: Oh, as I was busy admiring this vista, which prob'ly
no white man had ever seen before, he slipped down the
other side of the mountain, striving to take advantage of

my distraction, and put some territory between us. I was
in no way worried, as he'd slowed considerable, what with
the loss of blood and all. I'd've even lingered longer on the
top of Mount Tahoma, pixilated as I was on what I saw,
but that a blizzard commenced to blow out of nowhere and
forced me to decamp for more amiable climes.

HANNAH GYNT: And did you lose him in that blizzard?
Is that where it happened?

PEER: No, m'am. I did not lose that buck. Most men would
have been discouraged, but I persevered. I tracked him
through that raging blizzard, even though I couldn't see
my hand in front of my face, or feel my frozen feet. I
tracked that buck back down the mountainside, across a
dozen glaciers, and finally caught up to him at the edge
of a mighty cliff, a sheer precipice, an icy falls, a frozen
cataract—

HANNAH GYNT: At last! So now he's in your sight again,
trapped and no escape—

PEER: I was up above him on a ledge. I drew a bead,
took aim through the pelting snow, and fired!

HANNAH GYNT: Land's sake. And then what happened?

PEER: Exactly nothing.

HANNAH GYNT: Nothing? What on earth d'you mean,
nothing?

PEER: I mean nothing, nohow, diddly squat! My powder'd
gotten wet and my rifle misfired. The buck turned his head
and cocked an ear. He'd somehow heard—don't ask me
how—the click of the hammer through the howling storm,
and was making ready to bolt. So I hurled my worthless
weapon aside, threw myself off the ledge, landed upon the
buck's broad-beamed back, and grabbed onto his antlers
for dear life. He was so startled—

HANNAH GYNT: And who wouldn't be, I declare, some
damn fool jumped on top of you—

PEER: He leapt off the cliff, into thin air, and we sailed a
mile into space, falling faster and faster through the heart
of the storm. Everything was white, the wind was rushing
past, we were flying through the snow! Down! Down!
Down! We dropped through the clouds, we scattered

eagles, we passed so close to a lightning bolt I could have reached out and grabbed it! In fact, I did! Just plucked it! On impulse, without thinking—and then let go of that durned lightning bolt in a San Francisco second, but not before I'd burned an indelible zigzag scar across the palm of my hand—

*(He shows her his palm, which has a zig zag scar across it—*HANNAH *gasps.)*

HANNAH GYNT: My word! *Peer!*

PEER: A celestial souvenir of my escapade, and proof positive of my veracity. But I had no time to dwell upon the pain and sizzle of my poor mortified flesh! Down we fell, through the heavens, dropping faster and faster! Then the clouds cleared, and below us I could see our reflection in an icy lake, getting bigger and bigger, coming up fast! And then we hit! A mighty splash!

HANNAH GYNT: A mighty rude awakening!

PEER: The buck was so heavy, and we were dropping so fast, we plunged straight to the bottom of that freezing lake. Must've been a mile or more. I held my breath and hung on. Then we swam for the surface. My lungs were bursting! I was out of breath and growing dizzy. The world was turning black, my life swimming before my eyes, I thought of you—

HANNAH GYNT: Did you, Peer? Did you?

PEER: I did, Ma, I swear you were my last thought before I went to meet my maker.

HANNAH GYNT: Ah, that's sweet. But then what happened?

PEER: We were under water so long by the time we got back up to the surface a sheet of ice three feet thick had formed across it. The buck butted his head against the ice, once, twice, three times. I could feel him losing strength, giving up hope. I thought we were done for. With the last ounce of gumption I had in me, I jabbed my heels into his flanks, he bucked like a wild bronco, his antlers cracked the ice and split it open, we breached up into the blessed air and splashed ashore.

HANNAH GYNT: Thank heaven a second time, and a third. And then?

PEER: It was so cold and I was so tired and weak from my various travails, my clothes froze solid, my fingers blue, my poor palm sore as blazes from where I grabbed that piece of greasy lightning—

HANNAH GYNT: Yes, son? Yes?

PEER: I lost my grip, slipped off the buck, and he got away. Va-moosed , as it were.

HANNAH GYNT: Oh, Peer. You poor boy. What a shame. To come so close, and work so hard, and end up with nothing. Ain't that just like life?

PEER: Yup. Ain't it? Ain't it just?

(He nods solemnly, then grins. He can't help revealing his pleasure in putting over his story. She catches his smirk and knows she's been deceived. She swats him, angry.)

HANNAH GYNT: Liar! I swear. This lie just gets bigger and bigger every time you tell it. You ought to be ashamed of yourself. And double shame on me for believing even one word for a single second. Scamp! What about that scar?

PEER: Oh, this? I got this going over a barbed wire fence.

HANNAH GYNT: Besides, now I recollect. You didn't even make that story up, the boy and the buck, you got it out of some book of tall tales or other and embroidered it to suit you. You haven't been out hunting at all, have you? You've been hiding from Smitty. My son, the coward. Ever since he thrashed you within an inch of your scrawny life—

PEER: He ain't thrashed me. 'Case you're curious, I thrashed him.

HANNAH GYNT: Listen to him. Look what I raised. A brawler, a hooligan—

PEER: Ah, Ma, listen to you. Brawler or coward. You're in a tizzy either way. What happened between Smitty and me was less than nothing. He questioned my veracity, is all, and I had to put him in his place.

HANNAH GYNT: Imagine that. Someone questioning *your* veracity. Well, well, well.

PEER: Some folks are plain ignorant, Ma. The world's full of 'em.

HANNAH GYNT: Speaking of ignorant, a lot's happened since you been gone. I imagine you'll be wanting to change your clothes and have a bath—

PEER: And why would I want to do that?

HANNAH GYNT: Thought you might be wanting to go to Ingrid's wedding—

PEER: Ingrid's wedding? Ingrid's getting married? Since when?

HANNAH GYNT: To John Johnson—

(PEER *guffaws*.)

PEER: John Johnson? That square-head? That turnip farmer? That bald, herring-breathed half-wit? Now, who's the liar? 'Case you didn't know, Ingrid's in love with me.

HANNAH GYNT: Well, she may be in love with you, but she's marrying John Johnson. And you could have had her, dowry and all, her daddy one of the richest farmers in the Territory, but you're off galavanting across the countryside on the backs of bucks the likes of which ain't never been seen by sober folks and good Christians—

PEER: I don't believe you. Ingrid wouldn't marry that overgrown clod. His brain's no bigger 'n a barnacle. The man's slower'n a gooeyduck—and half as savvy.

HANNAH GYNT: It's true, so help me. The nuptials are fixing to commence. Down at the White Eagle. Go see for yourself, you don't believe me. The band ought to be striking up any time now—

(*Music in the distance*)

HANNAH GYNT: What'd I tell you?

PEER: Damn! Holy tarnation!

(*He rushes off. She calls after him.*)

HANNAH GYNT: Ain't you gonna bathe?

(*From off:*)

PEER: Had a bath just the month before last!

HANNAH GYNT: Peer, wait up! I'm comin' with you!

(PEER *rushes back on and scoops her up in his arms.*)

PEER: No, you ain't!

HANNAH GYNT: I have to keep an eye on you. See you don't make a fool of yourself, ruin the wedding.

PEER: I ain't gonna ruin her wedding. Just gonna have a little fun, that's all, and see what's what. Pay my respects. Now, hush.

(He hangs her from a nearby tree by a loop in the back of her dress. She struggles and flails.)

HANNAH GYNT: Now, damn you, boy. Put me down! Let me off this blasted tree! Peer! I'm warning you, boy! I'll blister your backside from here to San Francisco! Put me down, Peer! Put me down!

PEER: Such language. If you were me, I'd have to wash your mouth out with pine soap and pickle juice. Try not to struggle, Ma. You'll tear your dress, and fall from the tree and break your dainty ankle. I'll be back before dark to get you down. I'll bring you something from the wedding feast. Some cake perhaps. And meat, too, if there's any left. Have a good time. Get some rest. I'll see you alki, Ma, as the Duwamish say. By and by.

(He strolls off.)

HANNAH GYNT: Peer! Peer! Oh, that boy! Damn it, somebody get me down from here! Help! Help!

(A moment passes. She fumes. Then a Duwamish man, BAD OTTER, strolls on, sees HANNAH GYNT, considers a moment, sucks on his pipe.)

BAD OTTER: Hannah Gynt.

HANNAH GYNT: Bad Otter.

BAD OTTER: Your boy's put you up a tree again. Third time this month.

HANNAH GYNT: It's a phase he's going through. Would you mind giving a poor widow woman a hand, and get me down? I'm startin' to itch.

BAD OTTER: Sure.

(He helps her down. She dusts herself off.)

BAD OTTER: What's he up to this time?

HANNAH GYNT: Gone to get the Devil up at Ingrid Ingersoll's wedding.

BAD OTTER: Liable to get himself killed, doing that.

HANNAH GYNT: He's bound for a bad end and an early grave. I ought to leave him to his own fool devices. But I can't. He's all I have in this world. Ain't that a bitter pill? A lying wastrel, no-good ne'er-do-well, just like his drunken, cheatin', stealin', two-timin', double-dealin'-off-the-bottom-of-the-deck daddy— (*She starts off, stops, turns back and looks at him.*)

HANNAH GYNT: Bad Otter, you comin'? There's a band, the bride's family butchered a cow, and I hear tell the critter was still a year or two shy of being not quite the oldest surviving specimen of bovine north of the Columbia and west of the Rocky Mountains, so she may be just this side of edible if you chew hard enough and squint.

BAD OTTER: In other words, pure leather.

HANNAH GYNT: Still got all your own teeth?

BAD OTTER: Most of 'em.

HANNAH GYNT: Well, then, come along. You should do just fine. There's bound to be plenty of liquor, too, to choke old Bessie down, and, if I know my Peer, for dessert, plenty of fancy fisticuffs and fireworks galore.

(*She stomps off.* BAD OTTER *shrugs.*)

BAD OTTER: Why not?

(*He strolls off. The wedding music swells.*)

Scene Two

(*A clearing on a hillside overlooking the wedding.* PEER *looks wistfully down at the festivities below. Music and voices drift up the hill. Sounds like a good time.*)

PEER: Wish I had a drink. Course, there's plenty to drink down at Ingrid's wedding, and I'll be there soon enough. Still.

(*He picks at his clothes.*)

PEER: I swear. My clothes are held together with nothing more 'n spit and sunshine.

(*He slaps his clothes, raising clouds of dust.*)

PEER: I should have bathed. Entered in triumph and glory. Let Ingrid see the error of her ways. Break her heart. I'd take her back. If she begged. If she got down on her knees. These clothes. I should burn them. They'll laugh. They always do. The hell with them! A drink would help.

(*He hears voices, hides himself. Two* YOUNG LADIES *enter.*)

FIRST YOUNG LADY: He went around *bragging* he was Ingrid's *beau*. Can you *believe* it? Doesn't that beat *all*?

SECOND YOUNG LADY: You know, his father was the town *drunk*, and his mother—well, in her day, she was *known*, shall we say, for her *friendly* ways and her tender and charitable treatment of stranger and neighbor alike—

FIRST YOUNG LADY: No! You're joshing me. But she's so *old*. Must be forty if she's a day.

SECOND YOUNG LADY: She was a *scandal* in her youth. My mama told me his parents *had* to get married. In a hurry. Her father marched them to the preacher at the point of a *pitchfork*. And he himself was born not *six* months *after* the wedding. No wonder he turned out the way he did. And the reason his daddy *drank* so—

FIRST YOUNG LADY: Yes?

SECOND YOUNG LADY: He was never quite sure the boy was *his*. Didn't look a *thing* like him—

(*They exit, giggling and gossiping.* PEER *emerges with a scowl.*)

PEER: Wonder what poor bastard they were talking about? If I didn't know better—

(*He sits down, looks dreamily up at the clouds.*)

PEER: There's a stagecoach. And there's a steam engine, puffing across the prairie. And there's a clipper ship, out of San Francisco—bound for Rio 'round the Cape Horn. Look at the sails on that one! And there's Peer—Captain Peer to you, swabbie, dressed in a blue and gold uniform, brass buttons, and gold braid and a captain's hat! Yes, sir! There's Captain Peer, standing on the quarterdeck, issuing orders. Captain Peer, the Pirate King! Scourge of the Spanish Main! Arrrrggg! A parrot on one shoulder and a patch over one eye, which Captain Peer lost in the sack of Panama, 'case you're curious, in an epic duel across the parapets, waged under the blazing Caribbean sun before

thousands of onlookers, just Captain Peer and the Spanish
Commander, the shouts of the crowd, the clash of steel,
swords flashing in the sun, clothing slashed to ribbons,
back and forth they duel for hours, thrust and parry, blood
streaming from a hundred, no, a thousand wounds, large
and small, and Captain Peer, distracted momentarily by a
comely smile from a breathtakingly beautiful senorita on a
balcony strewn with roses, Captain Peer, ever the gallant
gentleman, tips his hat to pay his respects and
consequently stumbles on the cobblestones, the Spanish
Commander flicks the tip of his blade, so— and catches the
Captain's eye and slits it across, blood gushes from the
socket, the crowd gasps, grows silent, surely this is the end,
Captain Peer staggers, stumbles, stays on his feet, retreats,
the Spanish Commander smells victory, presses in for the
kill, Muerto! Muerto! he cries, slashing furiously with his
saber, Captain Peer blocks the blows, desperate, his vision
cloudy, the pain intense, searing, the sun dazzling, the sky
spinning, the Spanish Commander backs Captain Peer up
against a white-washed stone wall, pauses a moment, and
prepares to deliver the coup de grace, the crowd stunned
and silent, the only sound under the merciless sun the
labored breathing of the two swashbuckling combatants—
the Spanish Commander crosses himself, and then he
lunges, the crowd roars, a hoarse cry goes up from ten
thousand throats, Captain Peer dodges the blow, the blade
pierces his side but misses his heart, and Peer parries, like
this and that and thus and so—and stabs his sword square
through the Spanish Commander's neck—and sends him
straight to God! And the crowd erupts like a Roman
candle! Explodes! Runs amok! Goes hog wild and dances
famdangoes in the streets! Frenzy! Chaos! Church bells and
cannon fire! Flowers and hats fill the air! Never have they
seen such a fight! Such bravery! Such swordsmanship!
Such panache! They pick Captain Peer up and put him on
their shoulders and carry him to the plaza, where they tend
his wounds. And the most beautiful senorita in Panama,
in the Caribbean, in the whole of the Western Hemisphere
perhaps, she who favored him with a smile from the
balcony strewn with roses and so caused him to lose his
footing, this very same senorita insists on staunching his

ACT ONE

wounds and mopping his brow and lifting the water l
to his parched lips. And she smiles her incomparable s
and he thinks it well worth the loss of an eye. A mere
Small price to pay for such a smile. And she stays with him
through the sultry night, which is filled with the scent of
jasmine and the cries of nightingales and peacocks. And
in the morning he's well enough to travel, and she
accompanies him back to his ship, and the trade winds
billow the sails, and they lift anchor and set sail for a desert
isle of flowers and coconut palms, and together they count
out a fortune in Spanish gold and jewels, while she strums
a guitar and sings a gypsy ballad.

(He falls silent, daydreaming, lost in reverie.)

PEER: They still talk about it. Down in Panama. 'Case you
didn't know.

*(SMITTY, the local blacksmith, a burly fellow, and a couple of his
PALS, dressed in their Sunday best, stroll through the clearing on
their way to the wedding. SMITTY sees PEER.)*

SMITTY: Well, well, well. Look who's here. Little Peer.
I haven't seen you since I bloodied your nose. What was
that, six weeks ago now?

PEER: Don't flatter yourself. You must have been sore for
days, the thrashing I gave you.

SMITTY: My hands were sore. From hitting you on your
hard head.

(He and his friends laugh, which enrages PEER.)

PEER: Don't laugh, you ignoramuses!

SMITTY: Now I know why they call you a numbskull.
My hands were numb from drumming on your thick skull.

PEER: You're the thick one. You have a short memory,
to insult me this way. Fortunately for you, I'm in a good
mood today.

SMITTY: We're all in a good mood today. It's a festive
occasion. Ingrid's wedding. Have you heard? Were you
invited? Of course, you've been away. Tell me, where have
you been hiding these last six weeks? Ashamed to show
your face, I imagine.

PEER: Off having adventures the likes of which you could not possibly imagine.

SMITTY: Kidnapped by Sasquatch, eh? Or maybe the Haints of the forest got you. Took you to their lair, did they? Showed you their grisly doings? Slew a virgin or two before your very eyes? Boiled her up for stew?

PEER: I'm not going to waste my breath on a lunk like you.

SMITTY: Too bad. Nobody tells better whoppers than you, Peer Gynt, I'll give you that. You're an entertaining fellow. A first-class liar. I always stick up for you.

PEER: Thanks a bushel, Smitty.

SMITTY: Don't mention it. Folks say, that Peer Gynt, he's good for nothing, I say, you're wrong, you'll never find a better liar, search high or low, from here to Montana, nobody can lie like Peer. Makes the mountain men, as big a pack o' liars as ever graced God's green earth, seem as honest and plainspoken as primitive barefoot Baptist preachers.

PEER: It's your misfortune, and none of my own, that you're too dim to recognize the truth when you hear it. You're nothing but a country bumpkin.

SMITTY: And proud of it. Better a bumpkin than a daydreaming fool.

PEER: You were born in this dank and dismal wide spot in the road, and you'll die here too, covered with soot and smelling of horseshit.

SMITTY: And you. I suppose you're off to see the world, do great things, strike it rich and come back to lord it over us poor lugheads who stayed home and were dumb enough to do an honest day's work.

PEER: As a matter of fact, I am. Off to see the world. Strike it rich? Do great things? See if I don't.

SMITTY: Oh, sure you are. Alki, right, like the Indians say. By and by.

PEER: Sooner than you think.

(*A burst of music and voices from down the hill.*)

SMITTY: Wedding's about to get under way. Say. That reminds me. You were sweet on Ingrid, weren't you?

PEER: 'Case you'd care to be enlightened, Smitty. She was
sweet on me.

SMITTY: Threw you over for big John Johnson, didn't she?
Now there's a man. A real lumberjack. Taller 'n you by a
country mile, and shoulders like a wagon yoke. And the
village girls say he's big in every way. Tall timber, and rock
solid, if you get my meaning. With plenty o' sap.

(SMITTY *and his* PALS *laugh.*)

PEER: I wouldn't put much stock in village girls' gossip.

SMITTY: What your mama told me, and she should know.

PEER: Shut your mouth!

(PEER *rushes at* SMITTY *and takes a wild swing. Smitty's* PALS
grab PEER, *and* SMITTY *gives him a blow to the stomach that
leaves* PEER *writhing on the ground in pain.*)

SMITTY: More where that came from, if you dare to show
your ugly mug.

FIRST PAL: Ah, let him come to the party, Smitty. We could
use a good laugh. He can tell some of his tall tales, and
swear on a stack o' Bibles they're true. And we can guess
which book he stole 'em out of.

SMITTY: If that's your idea of fun—

FIRST PAL: Beats watchin' the grass grow—

SECOND PAL: Hey, Peer. Ingrid may be spoken for,
but there's plenty o' lonely widows in town, ain't too
particular. Maybe one o' them'd marry you. If you ask nice.

(*They laugh.* SMITTY *gives* PEER *a little kick.*)

SMITTY: I'll give your regards to the bride.

(*They walk off.* PEER *picks himself up and dusts himself off.*)

PEER: Now I'm really a sight. A bonafide ragamuffin.
I ought to go home and bathe. My poor clothes. Ingrid can
marry John Johnson, for all I care. The bitch. They deserve
each other. I wish I had a drink.

(*He starts. Listens. Looks around wildly.*)

PEER: Who's there? Is someone spying on me? I thought I
heard someone laughing. No. Maybe not. Just the wind in
the trees. Forest Haints. Spirits. The Duwamish say there's
a spirit lives in every stone—

(A burst of music stops him.)

PEER: I should go home. Get mother out of the tree.
She'll be madder 'n a wet hornet. I need a drink first.
And something to eat. And there'll be girls there, dozens
of them, each one prettier than the next, and all of them
prettier than Ingrid, that old sow. And they'll want to
dance with me. And hear where I've been. They'll have
missed me. Oh, Peer. Where have you been? Look at your
duds. You must have had some fabulous adventure.
Well—no, no. Nothing much. Just the usual. Hardly bears
repeating. Don't be shy. Come. Tell us all about it. Sit here.
Let us get you something to eat, to drink.

(He starts out.)

PEER: We've missed you so. Peer. We're wild for you.
Tell us everything. Show us your scar. Let me pull these
boots off. I'll rub your feet. There. Doesn't that feel better?
And later, when you're rested, and you've had enough to
eat and drink, we'll dance—

(He goes out. The music and sounds of the party come up.)

Scene Three

*(The courtyard of the White Eagle. The wedding celebration
swirls on. Music plays, the young folks dance. BAKER, the tavern
owner, seems to be the unofficial master of ceremonies. He shouts
to the crowd.)*

BAKER: Ain't this a barnburner? Eat! Drink! Dance! Enjoy
the hell outa yourselves! By the way— anybody seen the
preacher?

SMITTY: Passed out behind the bar.

BAKER: Hell and damnation. Somebody go slap him sober.

(SMITTY goes into the tavern.)

BAKER: Old reprobate.

FIRST WOMAN: We need a new preacher.

BAKER: Now, where we gonna get a new preacher?

FIRST WOMAN: Send away for one, I reckon. Mail order
from Boston.

BAKER: That'd take the better part of a year—

FIRST WOMAN: Maybe if we're lucky, this one'll get eaten by a bear.

BAKER: Then we'd *have* to get us a new preacher, wouldn't we? May I have this dance?

FIRST WOMAN: Certainly.

(They swirl off. Big JOHN JOHNSON *comes around the corner of the tavern, looking disconsolate. His* PA *sees him.)*

PA JOHNSON: Hey, Johnny, why the long face? I know you're getting married, but it ain't as bad as all that. At least try to smile for your Ma, she's awful upset—

JOHN JOHNSON: Ain't that, Pa. It's Ingrid.

PA JOHNSON: What's the matter? She got cold feet?

JOHN JOHNSON: I don't know. Maybe. She won't come out.

PA JOHNSON: Won't come out?

JOHN JOHNSON: No, sir. I tried talking to her, and all—

PA JOHNSON: Won't come out from where?

JOHN JOHNSON: Locked herself in the privy out back.

PA JOHNSON: Hell, son, they all do that. Last minute jitters. Getting the lace on her veil just so, or some such frimfram that means the world to them and we would not even notice less our feet were on fire. She'll be out once she feels better.

JOHN JOHNSON: She was crying, too. I could hear her. Somethin' fierce.

PA JOHNSON: Normal, normal, perfectly normal. 'Sides, we got time, the preacher ain't sober yet.

JOHN JOHNSON: He ain't? Oh, no—

PA JOHNSON: Now quit your caterwauling, let's go inside and see if we can pour some coffee down his gullet, it's gonna be alright—

JOHN JOHNSON: Okay, you say so. You sure? You sure, Pa?

(They go inside the tavern. FIRST *and* SECOND YOUNG LADIES *come rushing on.)*

FIRST YOUNG LADY: Here he comes, here he comes!

FIRST PAL: Here who comes?

SECOND YOUNG LADY: Peer Gynt! Peer Gynt!

SECOND PAL: He's got a lotta nerve. After Smitty laid down the law—

FIRST PAL: Now we'll have some fun. Get him going.
Get him to tell some o' his Peer Gynt whoppers.

SECOND YOUNG LADY: Oh, yes! Great fun! Get him going!
Wind him up and watch him rip!

(PEER *strides on, all puffed up with false bravado.*)

PEER: Ladies. Who wants to dance? Come on. Don't be shy.
How 'bout you?

FIRST YOUNG LADY: Not me, for sure, uh-uh, no sir,
not with you, Peer Gynt—

PEER: Your loss, and none of my own. Come on.
Who wants to shake a leg?

SECOND YOUNG LADY: I could be persuaded—

PEER: Come on then, step lively—

SECOND YOUNG LADY: But first I want to hear a story.

PEER: What kind of story?

SECOND YOUNG LADY: About you, Peer Gynt. About your
wild adventures and your supernatural magic powers—

FIRST YOUNG LADY: Your close scrapes and narrow
escapes—

SECOND YOUNG LADY: Your death-defying dare-devil
derring-do—

PEER: Don't you know how to turn a phrase? Girls after my
own heart.

SECOND YOUNG LADY: Then do tell. Do.

PEER: A *true* story? A hair-raising escapade? A saga that'd
shame the Norsemen? Well—nah, I'd rather dance. I'm in
a mood to cut a caper. Do a fancy step. Let's hop to—

FIRST PAL: Come on, Peer. Tell us how you can fly.
That's true, ain't it?

PEER: It's true. I can. Sail over the tree tops. Like a crow.

SECOND YOUNG LADY: Tell us how you can conjure the
spirits of the forest.

PEER: In two shakes of a lamb's tail. All the forest spirits, sprites—and the Haints, too. At my beck and call.

FIRST YOUNG LADY: The Haints. Oh, my. Ain't they dangerous?

PEER: You bet. Many's the man been hexed by Haints, taken sick and ruined.

SECOND PAL: Didn't I hear tell you had the cloak of invisibility? Makes a man disappear?

PEER: And the top hat, too. The top hat of invisibility. The cloak *and* the top hat. Look out I don't visit you in the night and snatch your life away. Mind how you treat me.

SECOND PAL: Ooo, I'm scared. I'm quaking. I'm in fear of my life.

(The crowd laughs. PEER *glowers.)*

PEER: Don't laugh! Don't laugh, damn you! If I had my pigsticker with me, you'd be laughing out the other side of your neck—

FIRST YOUNG LADY: Come on, Peer. They're only teasing. They're just jealous. What else can you do?

SEVERAL: Yes, tell us, Peer. Tell us what you can do.

PEER: Whatsoever you can imagine, and then some. I can make it rain. I can make the salmon run. Make 'em spawn before their time. I can make the corn grow tall and sweet, or put a curse on every ear, make every last kernel wither and blacken on the stalk. Best of all, I can summon up the Devil himself.

*(*BAKER *enters with a bottle of whiskey.)*

BAKER: So can my dear old sainted grandma, who used to do so on a regular basis. And so can any man, summon the Devil with a curse. But will he come when you do call? Old Scratch?

PEER: Every time. Once I lured him into a bottle. Tricked him. I won't say just how. May have to do it again someday. But I got him in there, and corked it up right after him, and you should've seen and heard how that old Devil carried on. Weeping and wailing and gnashing his teeth. Promised me all sorts of things. Earthly treasures. But I

wouldn't listen. I stuffed my ears and turned away.
I wasn't about to fall for his honeyed lies.

FIRST PAL: Look who's calling the Devil a liar.

SECOND YOUNG LADY: He's got gall, I'll give him that—

BAKER: Then you still got Satan, bottled up somewhere—

PEER: No, he got clean away.

FIRST PAL: *(Egging him on)* How'd he do that, Peer?

SECOND YOUNG LADY: Yeah, Peer, how'd that Devil get
away?

PEER: Well, I'll tell you. I put him on my shelf, for
safekeeping. And one day when I was out, Smitty came
around to do a chore for my Ma. And he picked that bottle
up, to see what was in it. And the Devil, knowing an easy
mark when he seen one, commenced to whisper sweet
nothings in Smitty's ear. And Smitty, being the gullible
type, with a fair amount of empty acreage suitable for
grazing where his brains oughta be, believed that old Devil,
and uncorked the bottle and let him out. And the Devil
unfolds himself in a sulfurous flash and stands before
Smitty, and the poor simpleton says, where's all that stuff
you promised me for helping you escape? And the Devil
says, come see me in Hell and I'll let you have it. And he
commences to vanish in a bigger flash than before. And
Smitty's sore he didn't get what he thought was coming to
him, and I'm sore Smitty let the Devil get away, and that's
why me and Smitty been quits ever since.

(Derision from the assembled multitude)

PEER: Although I imagine Smitty *will* get what's coming to
him, alki, as the Indians say, by and by.

FIRST PAL: What a liar!

FIRST YOUNG LADY: Some story!

SECOND YOUNG LADY: I've heard that tale before. My uncle
tells it every Halloween. Except it ain't a bottle, it's a
whiskey barrel—

SECOND PAL: My grandad tells it with a walnut shell—

FIRST YOUNG LADY: My grandma with a golden thimble—

FIRST PAL: Old as the hills and twice as dusty!

PEER: It's all true. And to hell with you what don't believe me.

(The crowd laughs in protest.)

PEER: No, it's true, damn you! If it weren't for Smitty's stupidity I'd have the Devil in a bottle to this very day.

FIRST PAL: *(To* SECOND PAL*)* Wait'll Smitty gets an earful of this latest slander.

SECOND PAL: Pepper Peer Gynt with buckshot and rock salt!

(The FIRST PAL *slips into the tavern.* BAKER *hands* PEER *the whiskey.)*

BAKER: Have a drink. Wet your whistle, long as you're here. You do spin an entertaining yarn, I'll give you that.

PEER: Thanks.

(He drinks deeply. Hands the bottle back to BAKER*. Sees* SALLY*, an attractive young woman standing on the edge of the crowd. Goes over to her.)*

PEER: What's your name?

SALLY: Sally.

PEER: Mine's Peer Gynt.

SALLY: I know. I heard about you.

PEER: What'd you hear?

SALLY: That you're the wild one.

PEER: It's true. I'm the wild one. Everything you hear about me is true. And then some. Want to dance?

SALLY: No. I can't.

PEER: Why can't you?

SALLY: I ain't allowed. My pa won't 'low me.

PEER: Won't 'low you to dance? Damn, that's strict—

SALLY: Won't 'low me to dance with *you*, Peer Gynt—

PEER: Me? Why not?

SALLY: I told you, you're the wild one—

*(*JOHN JOHNSON *and* PA JOHNSON *come out of the tavern.)*

JOHN JOHNSON: What're we gonna do? The preacher's too drunk to stand up straight, and the love of my life won't come out o' the crapper.

PA JOHNSON: Let's go find your Ma, maybe she can talk some sense into the girl.

JOHN JOHNSON: This ain't 'sposed to happen on a man's wedding day—

PA JOHNSON: Son, this is 'xactly the sort o' thing always happens on a man's wedding day—

(They go off.)

PEER: What's that? What're they talking about?

SALLY: Ain't you heard? This wedding's shaping up to be downright legendary.

PEER: How's that?

SALLY: Preacher Rowe's too stinko to say the ceremony, and the bride's gone and locked herself in the outhouse and won't budge, come hell or high water.

PEER: Ingrid?

SALLY: You know of another bride at this here wedding?

PEER: Hot damn! Come on, Sally, let's dance.

(He grabs her, they swirl around. PEER *dances faster and faster, swirling* SALLY *through the air, as his excitement grows.)*

SALLY: Whoa! Hey, Peer Gynt! Slow down, will you? What's the matter with you? Are you drunk, too?

PEER: Yes, I am. Drunk on you—

(She stops dancing and pulls away.)

PEER: What's the matter?

SALLY: I don't want to dance anymore. You scare me.

PEER: I'm sorry. Dance with me. Sally. I promise not to scare you.

SALLY: No. I'm going.

(She turns away. He grabs her arm.)

PEER: Don't go. Don't you dare spurn me, too. *(Threatening)* I'm a shape-shifter. I can shift myself into a frog, hop into your room, up on your bed and under your covers—

SALLY: Are you crazy? Let go of me!

PEER: Turn myself into a crow and sit outside your window all night long. Flap my wings against the windowpane, and caw your name. Make myself a haint and steal you away.

Become a blood-sucking bat, lap up your blood like a thirsty cat—

SALLY: Let go, get your hands off—

(She struggles. He suddenly lets go of her and runs off. SMITTY comes out of the tavern, looking for PEER.)

SMITTY: Where is he? Where'd he go?

SALLY: Who?

SMITTY: Peer Gynt, the lying bastard.

SALLY: I don't know.

(JOHN JOHNSON and his MA and PA come back through.)

MA JOHNSON: Honestly, John. It's a wonder you can get yourself dressed in the morning. I ain't surprised the poor girl's beside herself, thinking about what she's got in store, living with you the rest of her natural life—

JOHN JOHNSON: Ma—

(They go into the tavern. SMITTY takes off his jacket, hands it to one of his PALS, and rolls up his sleeves.)

SMITTY: He's been asking for it, now he's really gonna get it. I'm gonna make his square head ring like a hammer on a horseshoe.

(HANNAH GYNT and BAD OTTER enter.)

HANNAH GYNT: Sounds like my son you're talking about—

SMITTY: Miz Gynt, I'm afraid it is. I'm sorry, but Peer's got it coming. Called me stupid in front of my friends.

HANNAH GYNT: Simmer down, Smitty. I got first crack at Peer. Anybody else has got to wait in line.

SMITTY: He needs a good thrashing—

HANNAH GYNT: He'll get one from me, I guarantee—

SMITTY: Begging your pardon, m'am, but you're his mother, no offense. I'm the one to knock some sense into his thick skull.

HANNAH GYNT: Smitty, I beg to disagree—

(BAKER, PA JOHNSON and MA JOHNSON drag the dead-drunk PREACHER ROWE out of the tavern and attempt to prop him up.)

BAKER: Where's his hat? Anybody seen the Preacher's chapeau?

(Somebody picks up PREACHER ROWE's *trampled chapeau and hands it to* BAKER, *who sets it on* PREACHER ROWE's *head.)*

BAKER: Alright. Time to get this conflagration started!

(He fires his pistol several times in the air. This gets everyone's attention. The music stops. The crowd gathers round.)

BAKER: Open his hands. See he don't drop the Good Book—

(MA and PA JOHNSON open PREACHER ROWE's *hands. BAKER puts a Bible in his hands. PREACHER ROWE blinks, clearing cobwebs.)*

PREACHER ROWE: *(Thickly)* Dearly beloved—

BAKER: Not yet, Preacher, not yet. The bride and groom ain't here. Steady as she goes—

SMITTY: Here he comes! Here comes the groom! Here comes the lucky so-and-so!

(JOHN JOHNSON pushes his way through the crowd.)

JOHN JOHNSON: Ma! Pa!

MA JOHNSON: What is it, son?

JOHN JOHNSON: She's gone! She's gone! Ingrid's gone!

PA JOHNSON: What do you mean, gone? Gone where?

JOHN JOHNSON: I don't know. Just—gone!

(General commotion)

SMITTY: Let's form a search party! We'll find her, Mr and Mrs Johnson, don't you fear—

BAKER: Hold your horses. Let's not go off half-cocked. Maybe she don't want to be found.

JOHN JOHNSON: What're you getting at, Mr Baker?

BAKER: Some folks get cold feet at the very last minute. Specially brides. Been known to happen—

JOHN JOHNSON: No, no, it ain't like that. Ingrid wanted to get married. Was her idea—

BAD OTTER: *(Calmly)* There she is. Up yonder.

MA JOHNSON: Where?

(He points up the hill. The crowd looks where BAD OTTER points. They gasp.)

JOHN JOHNSON: It's Peer! Peer Gynt!

HANNAH GYNT: Oh, my God in Heaven! Preserve me!

PA JOHNSON: Well, I'll be a sorry son of a bitch!

JOHN JOHNSON: He's got Ingrid slung over his shoulder, like a sack of wet flour!

MA JOHNSON: He's done stolen the bride! I'll kill him!

BAKER: Boy's agile, I'll give him that. Scampering along the ridge there like a wild mountain goat. And Ingrid ain't exactly light as a feather quilt, beg your pardon Mrs J.—

MA JOHNSON: And just how would you happen to know that, Mr Barkeep Baker? Not from first-hand experience, I warrant—

BAKER: No, m'am. Just idle speculation—

MA JOHNSON: I'll thank you to keep your idle speculation to yourself—

PA JOHNSON: I'll tear him limb from limb! I'll skin him alive!

HANNAH GYNT: I'll never live this one down! I'm disgraced!

SMITTY: Let's go get him! Kidnapper! Bride snatcher! We'll tar and feather the little weasel! We'll hang him from the nearest tall cedar!

HANNAH GYNT: Not if I can help it! I got first dibs! He's mine! Everybody else, stand aside!

CROWD: Kidnapper! Bridesnatcher! After him! The scoundrel! Shape-shifting sonuvabitch! Let's go get him! Necktie party! Hang him high!

(Everyone, with the exception of BAD OTTER, *rushes out, leaving* PREACHER ROWE *with no visible means of support. He topples over.* BAD OTTER, *alone on stage with the comatose* PREACHER ROWE, *sucks on his pipe contemplatively, watching the posse go off in hot pursuit of* PEER. *He blows a couple of smoke rings.)*

BAD OTTER: Immigrants.

*(*PREACHER ROWE *stirs, sits up.)*

PREACHER ROWE: *(Thickly)* You may kiss the bride.

BAD OTTER: Wedding's over, Preacher.

*(*PREACHER ROWE *nods happily, belches once, and lies back down.)*

END ACT ONE

ACT TWO

Scene One

(In the mountains. Early morning. PEER *comes out of the forest.*
INGRID, *her bridal gown rumpled and torn, follows forlorn,*
clutching at him, and weeping.)

INGRID: Peer! What are you doing? Where are you going?
Wait for me—

PEER: Let go. Don't touch me. Leave me alone. Go away.

INGRID: Where'm I supposed to go?

PEER: Home.

INGRID: I can't go home.

PEER: Why not?

INGRID: You know why. I'm disgraced. I'm ruined.
I'm forlorn. I've been out all night. You and me—

PEER: Ain't my business.

INGRID: You deceived me—

PEER: You came with me willing, and eyes open. Now the
fun's over, and it's time we went our separate ways.

INGRID: No. We can't. We've committed a sin, in the eyes of
God. We're in this together.

PEER: Sin. Ain't that a laugh. You can go to hell, for all I
care. All women can go to hell. All but one—

INGRID: And who would that be?

PEER: Not you, that's for damn sure—

INGRID: Peer. Darling—

PEER: I ain't your darling—

INGRID: Why do you misuse me so? What am I supposed to do? First you seduce me. And then, after you had your way with me, you want to toss me aside like a dirty rag—

PEER: You came with me of your own free will, and I ain't had to twist your arm to do any of it. You were just looking for a handy crowbar to pry yourself outa that wedding, and I happened to fit the bill. Furthermore, it seems to me, I wasn't the only one had a pretty entertaining time last night—

INGRID: Oh, I did, Peer, I did, it was wonderful—

PEER: And taught me a thing or two I ain't known heretofore about the sophisticated arts of love. So quit your seduced and abandoned virginal carrying on. Ain't convincing.

INGRID: You're a fool you don't marry me, Peer Gynt.

PEER: Why's that?

INGRID: Well, besides the obvious, which you already had a taste of—and weren't it delicious?—you oughta get down on your knees and thank your lucky stars, my daddy's the richest man in the whole Puget Sound Territory, from Canada to the Columbia and both sides of the Cascades, and all his property would go to you, were you my lawful, wedded, loving husband—

PEER: No, thanks. I ain't aiming to stick around these parts too long. I got bigger fish to fry.

INGRID: Then the hell with you, Peer Gynt. You'll end up at the end of a rope, you leave me—

PEER: I'll take my chances.

INGRID: I could make you happy. Wealthy and respectable—

PEER: I don't deserve that. Ain't worth it—

INGRID: You led me on!

PEER: You wanted to come. You were eager.

INGRID: I was desperate!

PEER: And I was crazy, must've been, get mixed up with the likes of you. Hysterical woman—

INGRID: You'll regret this, Peer Gynt.

PEER: Not near as much as I'd regret marrying you every day for the rest of my life.

INGRID: Well. We'll see. We'll see what becomes of this sorry business.

PEER: Guess so. Guess we will.

(She starts out. PEER shakes his head.)

PEER: Women.

(She stops and turns back to look at him.)

INGRID: All but one.

PEER: That's right. All but one.

INGRID: Lucky girl. Wonder who she is.

(PEER shrugs, doesn't answer. After a moment, they go their separate ways.)

Scene Two

(HANNAH GYNT, SALLY, and BAD OTTER are wandering through the mountains, searching for PEER and INGRID. A storm is brewing.)

HANNAH GYNT: That boy's been an aggravation to me since the day he came into this world.

BAD OTTER: Some are born restless under a wandering star.

HANNAH GYNT: Trouble follows him, that's for sure. *(Reading sky)* Weather's coming. We have to find him 'fore nightfall. 'Fore the others do. If the storm don't kill him, the posse will. God help me, he's my flesh and blood, my very own, and I cannot raise a hand against him, much as I might like to, whatever his crimes. *(To SALLY)* I can't believe what he's gone and done. If I hadn't seen it with my own eyes, you'd never've convinced me in a month of Sundays. He's been all talk heretofore, all talk and tales fantastical. Wool-gathering and yarn-spinning, and enough hot-air to power a steam locomotive clear across the country. And now, for the first time in his life, don't ask me why, he's up and *done* something, 'stead of just talking about it, and, wouldn't you know it, it's like to get him hanged. His Daddy run off when Peer was nothing much more than a new-hatched fingerling. So it's just been me and him, always. And we'd keep company around the fire, and while away the winter rains, telling tales. Fairy tales, mostly. Ghost stories. Children grow up and leave such nonsense behind, except as stuff to pass the time with their own young 'uns. But not Peer. It stuck with him, spooks and goblins, witches and devils and Haints, and things that go bump in the night. Come to think of it, there was a tale he always cottoned to about a boy who steals a bride—

(She shakes her head, despairing. Surveys the country below.)

HANNAH GYNT: Not a trace of my son. It's like the earth swallowed him up. He's lost.

BAD OTTER: There *are* spirits. In the trees and stones. In the creeks and rivers. Maybe Peer knows more 'n most white folks.

HANNAH GYNT: Bad Otter. Don't you go talking that Duwamish mumbo jumbo to me. I'm a good Christian woman and will have none o' that. Still and all, maybe I've been too hard on the boy. Maybe he told more truth than I ever gave him credit for. Maybe he can come through all this tribulation, come through it unscathed.

SALLY: What do you mean?

HANNAH GYNT: Maybe he ain't lied when he said he could fly. Or turn himself invisible. Maybe he really can. I hope so. For his sake. Otherwise, he's done for.

BAD OTTER: Stay here and rest. I'll search down below for some sign.

(He goes. SALLY and HANNAH GYNT sit.)

HANNAH GYNT: Getting dark. Wind's coming up. It's going to rain like the end o' the world tonight. Bad Otter's right. There are spirits in these mountains. And that's a fact. The Good Lord help my boy. If the posse don't get him, the Haints surely will.

SALLY: Tell me more about him. About your son.

HANNAH GYNT: Peer? What do you want to know?

SALLY: Everything. All there is to know.

HANNAH GYNT: If I were to tell you all there is to know about my child, I'd wear you out, long before I got to the end of the telling. He is the most remarkable boy, in spite of all his faults.

SALLY: Try me. Talk as long as you please. You'll lose your voice before I grow weary of listening to you talk about Peer Gynt.

HANNAH GYNT: Caught your eye, has he?

SALLY: Captured my interest, you might say.

HANNAH GYNT: Well, let's see.

(HANNAH GYNT *arranges herself and takes* SALLY's *hand.*)

HANNAH GYNT: He learned to talk at a godawful early age—

SALLY: Fancy that—

HANNAH GYNT: And his first words, I'll never forget, right off the bat, were "Ma, you know what I just seen?"— followed by a full-blown yarn, 'bout a snappin' turtle, a grizzly bear, a pot o' gold, assorted pirates—and Coyote, the Trickster—

(*As* HANNAH GYNT *tells* SALLY *her story of* PEER, *the wind comes up, and the storm blows the next scene on.*)

Scene Three

(*A clearing. Late in the day.* PEER *appears.*)

PEER: Posse's after me. The whole damn town. Half the territory. Ingrid's father'd see to that. What do I care. Let 'em try 'n string me up. (*Takes a deep breath*) This is it! This is the life! Ain't I an outlaw! A wanted man! A dangerous desperado! I'm stronger, faster, 'n smarter than they are! See if I ain't! I'm a grizzly bear, a mountain lion, a bald eagle! I'm the King of the Salmon, wily and free! And the hell with all my worthless, no-good lies! Now I've gone and *done* something! At last! Now, I can live!

(*Three* FERAL GIRLS *appear at the edge of the clearing. They eye* PEER. *They're wild, savage, dirty and half-naked, dressed in rags.*)

FIRST FERAL GIRL: There's a one. Pretty boy—

SECOND FERAL GIRL: Looks plump enough.

THIRD FERAL GIRL: Maybe he'll do for a light snack.

SECOND FERAL GIRL: I'm feeling peckish, how 'bout you?
(They laugh.)

PEER: And what the hell are you three?

THIRD FERAL GIRL: What are we?

FIRST FERAL GIRL: We live here—

SECOND FERAL GIRL: In these mountains—

PEER: Nobody lives here. Not even Indians. There's only spirits and Haints up this high—

THIRD FERAL GIRL: We do. Amongst the wild things—

(They surround him.)

SECOND FERAL GIRL: And we ain't spirits—

FIRST FERAL GIRL: Touch us, you don't believe we're real—

(They touch him. He touches them back.)

THIRD FERAL GIRL: What do you think? Eh, boy? Do we feel like spirits to you?

PEER: Nope. Feel like the real McCoy. Like flesh and blood girls.

SECOND FERAL GIRL: Oh, we're that, alright. We're flesh and blood girls—

PEER: You ain't Haints?

THIRD FERAL GIRL: We're exactly what we appear to be—

FIRST FERAL GIRL: Pretty boy, care to pass the time with us?

THIRD FERAL GIRL: Ever been with a woman, pretty boy?

PEER: Oh, sure, lots of times. Whenever I want—

SECOND FERAL GIRL: Oh, sure you have—

THIRD FERAL GIRL: Whenever you want—

PEER: I have, it's true. Whenever I want. They come begging—

FIRST FERAL GIRL: Ever been with three at once?

(PEER starts to answer, hesitates. No, some lies are too big, even for him.)

PEER: Uh, no. No, I can't say that I have. I have done a lot o' things in my life, but never that. Never more 'n one woman at once.

SECOND FERAL GIRL: Could be your fortune's changed this day.

PEER: No doubt about it, I'd say. You three got men?

FIRST FERAL GIRL: We did, but—

THIRD FERAL GIRL: Not no more.

PEER: What happened to 'em?

FIRST FERAL GIRL: Mine left me for a merry widow—

SECOND FERAL GIRL: Mine ran off with some fortune-telling gypsy—

THIRD FERAL GIRL: Mine was a card-sharp and got what was coming to him.

PEER: Strung up?

THIRD FERAL GIRL: Shot between the eyes. They kicked over his chair and kept on playing.

FIRST FERAL GIRL: So, you see, we're all alone—

SECOND FERAL GIRL: We're lonely. Stay with us—

FIRST FERAL GIRL: Pretty boy—

THIRD FERAL GIRL: Pretty boy, spend the night with us—

FIRST FERAL GIRL: Spend the night in our arms—

SECOND FERAL GIRL: Are you man enough for three?

FIRST FERAL GIRL: Are you?

THIRD FERAL GIRL: Man enough?

SECOND FERAL GIRL: For three?

PEER: More 'n man enough for all of you. I'm a man and a half! Try me—

FIRST FERAL GIRL: Alright, I think I will—

(She kisses him.)

FIRST FERAL GIRL: Yum! He's delicious!

SECOND FERAL GIRL: Let me try!

(They take turns kissing and caressing him.)

FIRST FERAL GIRL: Sweeter 'n wild huckleberries!

THIRD FERAL GIRL: Purely succulent, I'd say!

SECOND FERAL GIRL: Hotter 'n a branding iron!

FIRST FERAL GIRL: And just as hard!

THIRD FERAL GIRL: Stronger 'n a young stallion in spring fever!

(Laughing, they start to lead him off.)

PEER: Where're you taking me?

FIRST FERAL GIRL: Paradise, you silly boy. Don't you wanna go?

PEER: With all my heart.

SECOND FERAL GIRL: Then get a move on! Don't dawdle!

THIRD FERAL GIRL: We have food and drink and a warm fire. And three soft beds for you to choose from.

PEER: I choose them all!

FIRST FERAL GIRL: Pretty boy!

(They laugh and rush out.)

Scene Four

(Sunset the next day. A storm rumbles on the horizon. The snow-capped mountains are rosy in the dying light. PEER enters, drunk and dishevelled.)

PEER: Oh, my head! It hurts! Damn! Every vein throbs.
I think I have a fever. I hear bells. The light is so beautiful.
Like roses. The mountains look like icy castles. Now they're
on fire. I must lie down. Oh, my aching head. *(He lies down.)*
Did I really steal a bride and carry her away into the
mountains? A posse howling at my heels? Did I really
leave the bride behind and spend a day and a night
frolicking with three wild women of the mountains?
Like to wear a man out, those three. Kill him with kindness.
Seems like a dream. Must have been a lie. A tall tale.
A damn lie and a damn shame. Oh, my head hurts!
I'm seeing things. Those shadows look like soldiers—
(He looks upwards.) There's a pair of eagles soaring over
yonder gorge. Wonder where they're going? Look at them.
Free. Free as a bird, that's what they say. And I'm stuck
here on the ground, with all my trials and tribulations.
(He gets to his feet.) I can do like them eagles. Soar like that.

Ride the four winds. Go where fortune and fancy take me.
The girls I leave behind will wait in vain for my return.
Pace along the widow walk. Scan the horizon. Pine away.
I won't be back. The four winds, the seven seas. I will know
them like most men know their front parlor. *(Stares out)*
Funny. That cloud there looks like my granddaddy's farm.
Like it was when it was first hacked out of the howling
wilderness and wrought like Spanish silver into something
fine. Not the sorry heap of scraps it is now, but shining and
new, full of light and music and people laughing. There's
a party, a celebration! A new-born boy! They drink his
health! To Peer, my daddy says! To Peer! All the leading
citizens of the Territory gather round and drink to me!
To my future! To Peer! Whose daddy was a dandy!
To Peer! Born of a great family! And destined for fame
and fortune!

(Lightning crackles, thunder claps. PEER stands on the precipice, arms outstretched.)

PEER: Peer Gynt! Peer Gynt! Peer Gynt!

(A bolt of lightning hits him, knocks him out cold.)

Scene Five

(A starry night. A hillside. A WOMAN IN GREEN, wearing a velvet hooded cape, comes in, followed by PEER, who pants after her like a lovesick dog. She turns to him, pulling her hood back to reveal her brilliant shiny metallic green hair.)

WOMAN IN GREEN: Are you telling me the truth? You love me?

PEER: I do. Sure as your hair is green as emeralds. Sure as my name is Peer Gynt. Sure as the night is black and starry. Sure as you're the most beautiful woman I've ever seen.

WOMAN IN GREEN: You just want someone to cook for you.

PEER: Nope. Nor clean, nor scrub floors, neither, nor put up loganberry jelly and fig preserves, nor slop hogs, nor water chickens, nor butcher wild game. None o' that. I'll treat you kind, you'll see. Won't you have me? I'll stuff you full of sugarplums—

WOMAN IN GREEN: You'll beat me, won't you? I know your type.

PEER: Never fear, beautiful lady, I come from royal blood. Noble lineage. We never beat our women, we treat 'em right, handle 'em with kid gloves—

WOMAN IN GREEN: Noble lineage, huh? Who's your daddy?

PEER: King Jedediah of Gynt. I'm a prince. 'Case you didn't know.

WOMAN IN GREEN: Well, it just so happens, I'm a princess!

PEER: No!

WOMAN IN GREEN: Yes!

PEER: You don't say!

WOMAN IN GREEN: I do indeed!

PEER: Well, ain't that a coincidence!

WOMAN IN GREEN: Don't it beat all?

PEER: You see? It's a match made in heaven! You and me! It's destiny! Who's your pa?

WOMAN IN GREEN: The King of the Mountains. 'Case you didn't know.

PEER: I thought the King of the Mountains was Paul Bunyan. And his blue ox, Babe.

WOMAN IN GREEN: My daddy makes Paul Bunyan look like a pipsqueak. Makes Babe look like a lame lap dog.

PEER: That's remarkable!

WOMAN IN GREEN: You should see my daddy's palace. High in the ice and snow, dead center in the furthest reaches of the Olympic Peninsula, beyond seven times seven mountain ranges, each one higher than the last, where no pioneer nor Indian even has ever yet set foot. In fact, it's right at the very very top—of the Big Rock Candy Mountain!

PEER: The Big Rock Candy Mountain!

WOMAN IN GREEN: The very very top! Near the Lemonade Springs!

PEER: Where the bluebird sings? That's remarkable! You should see my ma's palace. It's something to behold,

I can tell you. It's most splendiferous! You'd just have to see it to believe it—

WOMAN IN GREEN: I would, would I?

PEER: Take your breath away.

WOMAN IN GREEN: My daddy's name is King Clem. Heard of him?

PEER: My ma's name is good Queen Hannah. Heard of her?

WOMAN IN GREEN: My daddy stomps his foot, crevices open in the earth, and avalanches pour down the mountain sides!

PEER: My ma pitches a fit, glaciers break off and fall into the sea! Grizzly bears whimper like sick pups! Cougars crawl off to die!

WOMAN IN GREEN: My daddy can leap from mountaintop to mountaintop, easy as schoolgirls hopscotch!

PEER: My ma can swim like a salmon and run like an antelope and sing as sweet as any coyote!

WOMAN IN GREEN: Are those pitiful rags your Sunday go to meeting clothes?

PEER: I only wear these humble duds because you couldn't look upon my Sunday best, the sight would strike you blind.

WOMAN IN GREEN: This cloak is spun from emeralds, which my daddy has in such abundance he grinds 'em up like so much cornmeal!

PEER: Looks like cheap second-hand hand-me-down two-dollar whore's velvet to me, you don't mind my saying so. A bit the worse for wear.

WOMAN IN GREEN: I know. But things ain't ever what they seem to be with us. Where I come from, everything has a double nature. They're just the opposite of what they appear to be. For instance, when you see my daddy's palace, you'll think it's the most run-down tar-paper country shack you ever laid eyes on. And instead of high on the very very top of the Big Rock Candy Mountain, which is where it is, for sure, and that's a fact, you'd say it was stuck out in the middle of the most miserable godforsaken muskrat swamp west of the Mississippi.

But that's 'cause we put a spell on it, to keep it safe from those who'd do us harm.

PEER: Same with us, I know just what you mean. Double nature. We're fixed up that way, too. We got stacks of gold coins in our house disguised as mouse droppings. Sheets of silver you'd take for rusty old pie plates. And crystal windows that appear to be for all the world old yellow newspapers instead of leaded glass.

WOMAN IN GREEN: Double nature. Black is white, and white is black, and pretty's plain and plain's pretty. And uglier than sin is plumb, dumb beautiful.

PEER: Young is old, and old is new. Hot is cold, and cold is hot. North is south, and south is north.

(She throws her arms around him and gives him a kiss.)

WOMAN IN GREEN: Oh, Peer, I knew we'd hit it off! We were meant to be together!

PEER: Like beans and rice! Like gravy and biscuit! Like moonshine and a jelly jar!

WOMAN IN GREEN: Let's go see my daddy!

PEER: How we gonna get all the way to the Big Rock Candy Mountain? That's dead center in the middle of the Olympic Peninsula, a hundred miles west of here. Across seven times seven mountain ranges, each one higher'n the last—

WOMAN IN GREEN: Don't fret, honey. I got that difficulty licked.

(She whistles. Winks at PEER.*)*

WOMAN IN GREEN: Get a load of this, sugar.

(A GIANT RACOON *ambles in, with a saddle on its back. The* WOMAN IN GREEN *hops on and grabs the reins.)*

PEER: Will you look at that? Shades of Pecos Bill, I swear.

WOMAN IN GREEN: Hop on, honey. Let's git some gone! We're going home to the King of the Mountains! To the very very top of the Big Rock Candy Mountain! Where the bluebirds sing at the lemonade springs, and never is heard a discouraging word, and the skies are not cloudy all day—and get hitched!

PEER: Suits me.

*(*PEER *clambers aboard behind her.)*

WOMAN IN GREEN: Peer, honey, I was feeling kinda sad and blue 'til you came along. Just goes to show, *c'est la vie*, say the old folks, it goes to show you never can tell.

PEER: Nope. You never can. Let's head for the hills! Giddyup!

WOMAN IN GREEN: Yahoo!

(The GIANT RACCOON *starts out.)*

PEER: Hot damn! My ma always told me, you can tell a man's class by the caliber of his transportation. If this don't beat all.

(They exit.)

Scene Six

(The lair of the KING *of the Mountains: a ramshackle swamp cottage made of mud, muck and sticks, deep in a damp, mosquito-ridden swamp in the furthest reaches of the Olympic Mountains. The* KING *himself is a dirty, ragged, leering little one-eyed drunken Haint, and his subjects are also Haints—a motley, drooling collection of deformed, lecherous, inbred witches who, at the moment, are howling for the blood of* PEER, *who stands pale and terrified before the* KING. *The* WOMAN IN GREEN *is off to one side, wiping away tears. The* KING *sits in a broken-down chair, picking his teeth with a hunting knife, while various* HAINTS *of both sexes dance around* PEER, *poking at him, and howling in his face.)*

FIRST HAINT: Look at him! He makes my skin crawl!

SECOND HAINT: He's deformed! His mother musta had congress with a multitude of mountain goats to beget such a mangy specimen!

THIRD HAINT: Who does he think he is, taking filthy liberties with the daughter of the King!

FIRST HAINT: Varmint! Muskrat!

FOURTH HAINT: Hanging's too good for him!

FIRST HAINT: We oughta tar and feather him!

FIFTH HAINT: We oughta skin him alive!

SECOND HAINT: Flay him! Dress him out!

THIRD HAINT: Pour salt and vinegar on him!

FIFTH HAINT: Then tar and feather him!

FIRST HAINT: Cut off his dingleberry and stuff it down his throat! Make him choke on it!

THIRD HAINT: Couldn't choke a baby turkey on that shriveled-up bit of nothin' in particular!

SECOND HAINT: Stake him out naked on a red ant hill! Then cut it off!

HAINTS: Hang him! Skin him! Tar and feather! Cook him 'til he's done! Cut off his dingleberry and stuff it down his throat! Feed him to the coyotes!

(The KING holds up his knife to quiet the bloodthirsty crowd.)

KING: Alright, now. That'll be enough of that—

(They pay no attention. The FIRST HAINT continues to menace PEER.)

FIRST HAINT: I'd like to do to you what you did to our poor princess, see how good you like it, pokin' and pryin' where you don't belong—

(The KING pulls out a pistol and shoots the FIRST HAINT dead. This quiets the crowd.)

KING: Enough, I said. Pitch that stinking carcass in the swamp.

(Two of his minions pick up the body of the FIRST HAINT and haul it offstage. A satisfying kerplop is heard. The KING fixes his one good eye on PEER.)

KING: So this is the sorry critter wants to marry my daughter. Give me one good reason I shouldn't have your guts with my grits for breakfast. Prob'ly taste greasy like possum—

PEER: Well, Your Highness, I—

KING: If you're expecting some kinda dowry, don't count your chickens before they're hatched out. You ain't getting squat from me before I kick the bucket. Savvy?

PEER: Plain as day, Your Highness.

KING: Lemme see your feet.

PEER: Beg your pardon, King?

KING: Kick off your shoes, lemme take a gander at your nether hooves. And be quick about it—

PEER: Yes, sir, Your Highness, sir—

(PEER *kicks off his shoes.*)

KING: Hold 'em up here, lemme get a good look—

(PEER *does that, and the* KING *recoils from the smell.*)

KING: God Almighty, boy, ain't you ever washed them nasty things?

PEER: I meant to, sir. I've been busy.

KING: We ain't what you'd call fastidious in these here parts, but them things smell worse 'n a hide hunter knee-deep in bison gore.

PEER: Yes, sir.

(*The* KING, *keeping his ginger distance, examines* PEER's *feet.*)

KING: Well, you ain't got no webbing between your toes—

PEER: No, sir—

KING: Nor extra toes neither—

PEER: No, sir—

KING: And that worries me. Worries me sick. Makes me question your choice of kinfolk. Most folks around here got one or the other feature, if not both. Leave it to my daughter to pick herself an outsider ain't like us. If I had my druthers —put your shoes back on, son—if I had my druthers, she'd marry kin. The closer the better, far as I'm concerned. You marry strangers, you buy a pig in a poke, like my mama, who was also my aunt and some kinda second cousin, always told me. But not my daughter— who's also my niece, I believe. No, she had her mind made up, some damn fool idea. Coulda had her pick of cousins—

WOMAN IN GREEN: Daddy, all my cousins are backward. They're coarse. They're hairy.

KING: What about your brother Neal? Or your uncle Zachariah?

WOMAN IN GREEN: Even worse. They both look like they been rode hard and put away wet.

KING: (*To* PEER) Fine men, both of 'em. And more's the point, family. So she drags you home—looking like

something you scrape off your boots, not have to supper—
and expects the red carpet to come rolling out and a brass
band to serenade the happy couple. Well, before she twists
her old pap's arm, I got a couple of items I wanna get
straight with you, young fella.

PEER: Go ahead, Your Highness. Shoot.

KING: These items are not up for grabs, if you get my drift.
You got to follow 'em to the letter, and all of 'em. You fail
to adhere to these, deal's dead. Deader 'n a doornail.

PEER: I understand.

KING: And so are you.

PEER: Yes, sir. I understand. Dead, sir. Doornail, sir. Which
rules and regulations exactly did you have in mind?

KING: First and foremost, you got to put all thoughts of life
beyond these mountains out of your mind. You ain't never
going back to what you left behind, and you might as well
get that straight, and right away, 'cause you're quits with
your old life as of this very moment, and that's the truth.

PEER: As far as my old life goes, hell, it weren't much
anyway, mostly lies and prevarications, and I'm sure I
won't miss it once I'm married and sitting where you're
sitting.

KING: Don't get your britches in an uproar to take my
place, young buck. I ain't in no hurry to go to the happy
hunting grounds, I can tell you that.

PEER: What's the next thing? Hell, this is a piece of cake,
so far. Ducks in a barrel.

KING: Next thing? Oh, yeah. I got a hankering to know how
smart you are.

PEER: Plenty smart.

KING: Then riddle me this: when is a hawk like a handsaw?

PEER: You got me there. I'm stumped. Better string me up.
(*To* WOMAN IN GREEN) Looks like I'm a goner. (*To* KING)
Can I kiss the bride goodbye?

WOMAN IN GREEN: *Daddy.* No one knows the answer to
that riddle. Ask another—

KING: That's a hard one, I'll grant ye. I was hoping you had
the answer. 'Cause I used to know and I plumb forgot, and

it's driving me crazy. Let's see. Oh, yeah. You know the old saying, to thine ownself be true?

PEER: I believe I do.

KING: In these parts, we say, "Do what you gotta do", to get through.

(*The* HAINTS *chortle and guffaw.*)

SECOND HAINT: Do what you gotta do to get through. That's rich.

(PEER *scratches his head.*)

KING: You follow me, young fellow?

PEER: Well, Your Highness, I can't truthfully say that I do—

KING: You gotta engrave them words on the rotten wood of your shriveled heart if you're ever to rule over the Big Rock Candy Mountain. Do what you gotta do to get through!

PEER: Well, what the hell, when have I ever truthfully said? Do what you gotta do—

HAINTS: To get through!

(*The* HAINTS *cheer and applaud.*)

KING: That's fine. And to seal that oath, you'll drink our ale—

PEER: 'Twould be my pleasure.

(*One of the female* HAINTS *brings* PEER *a shabby wooden bowl, full of a foul steaming liquid.*)

KING: That bowl's gold. Solid gold.

PEER: I can see that. Might pretty, too. The shine fair hurts my eyes. Excuse me, but—this ale's—*hot*, Your Highness.

KING: Cold as hoarfrost. Straight from the lemonade springs! Drink!

(PEER *puts the bowl to his lips, takes a sip, grimaces and spits it out.*)

PEER: Begging your pardon, sir, but this ale tastes like cow piss! Smells like it, too—

KING: Now you know our secret. That's what we make our ale outa. The finest cow piss and a drop of blood, to savor. Tasty, ain't it. Now, sonny, if you know what's good for you, you'll drink, and drink deep.

(PEER *drinks it down in one gulp, then retches.*)

KING: Did I see you retch back up our finest ale?

PEER: Only so that I might taste it a second time,
Your Highness.

KING: Good answer. Now, you'll have to strip off those
rags and dress like we do.

PEER: When in Rome—

(*He starts to strip off his clothes. One of the female* HAINTS
*brings him some really foul swamp rags. He reluctantly puts
them on.*)

PEER: 'Bout as easy as falling off a log. You got anything
hard you want me to do? Your Highness?

KING: Nothing much. Come here. Let me have a look at
you.

(PEER *finishes putting on the swamp rat clothes and approaches
the* KING.)

KING: Now you look like one of us. You drank our ale,
you sealed the oath, you put on the suit o' lights, you're
just about fit to be my son-in-law. Sit down here beside me.
Darlin'! Let's have a song!

(*Everyone settles back, expectantly. Someone strums an out of
tune guitar. The* WOMAN IN GREEN *steps forward, slips off her
wig. She's bald.* PEER *is taken aback. The* WOMAN IN GREEN
*warbles and shrieks some ancient folk song, in some ancient
unknown language. Everyone but* PEER *is entranced.
She finishes. The* HAINTS, *led by the* KING, *applaud wildly.
The* WOMAN IN GREEN *curtsies, puts her wig back on.*)

KING: Tell me, future son-in-law. What did you think of
that? Some singing, eh? What a warbler!

PEER: Brought tears to my eyes, Your Highness—

KING: Mine, too. That's a damn famous aria, from some
Italian opera or other—

PEER: So that's what Italian sounds like—a pair of cats
making kittens.

KING: Well, opera ain't for every taste. It's elevated. You'll
catch on, in time. Tell you something. You're a lucky man.
The girl cooks just as good as she sings. And ain't she
beautiful?

PEER: She's sure enough bald.

KING: You ain't muttering a discouraging word, is you?
I can see you ain't entirely left your old life behind.
You still ain't seeing double-nature. I believe I can
remedy that—

(*He grabs* PEER *by the hair and takes aim with his knife.
The crowd howls.* PEER *resists.*)

PEER: What? What? What are you doing?

KING: I have to put out your eye, my son. Have to. So you
can see the world the way we see it. Aslant and askew,
upside down and inside out. With double nature, as in a
travelling sideshow mirror. It's for your own good, believe
me. You'll be happier this way, trust me.

PEER: Oh, I don't think so. Is this really necessary? I like my
eyes. Both of them—

KING: It is if you want to be King. Hold still, dammit!
I don't wanna slip, and cut off your nose—man needs his
nose—

(*The* KING *presses closer with his knife.* PEER *struggles in his
grasp. The crowd chants:*)

HAINTS: His eye! His eye! Put it out! Put it out!

PEER: No! Don't! Please! Don't put out my eye!

KING: Quit your bellayching! It'll feel good! I promise!
And the world will look ever so much better!

PEER: No! God damn it, stop! Let me go!

(*He wrenches free.*)

PEER: You're a crazy old coot!

KING: You're the one who's crazy, boy. Pass up the
opportunity to be King. How many men get a chance
to wear a crown?

PEER: King of what, I'd like to know? King of this
mosquito-ridden, godforsaken, fever-infested swamp?
King of a bunch of inbred, webfooted village idiots?
King of the Haints?

KING: Haints? Why, you're mistaken, son. Ain't no Haints,
here. Just simple country folk. Your vision's cloudy, and
your mind's deranged. If you'd just let me put out your
eye—

(A couple of HAINTS *grab* PEER *and hold him. The* KING *advances, knife poised.)*

KING: You'd soon see this place is paradise on earth! The finest shining country in all the Golden West!

PEER: I'm sure you're right. Paradise on earth. And more 'n I deserve. So I'll just be going now—

KING: Not so fast. I told you—there's no leaving here. It's Katie Bar the Door. You'll marry my daughter or die.

PEER: Alright. If you put it that way—I'll pledge my troth. Before we tie the knot, I have something I have to tell the blushing bride. And I'd like to do it before you take my eye, if you don't mind. The pain might make me lose my train o' thought—

KING: Say your piece and be quick about it.

(The HAINTS *turn* PEER *so that he can face the* WOMAN IN GREEN.*)*

WOMAN IN GREEN: Yes, darling.

PEER: I have something to tell you, dearest.

WOMAN IN GREEN: Hurry and tell me, darling, so that Daddy can put out your eye, and we can get hitched!

PEER: I ain't no prince.

(The crowd gasps.)

WOMAN IN GREEN: You ain't?

PEER: Nope. My pa ain't no king, and my ma ain't no queen, and I ain't got no gold nor silver, neither. I am just a poor boy, a long way from home—

(The WOMAN IN GREEN *screams a bloodcurdling banshee scream and faints dead away. The* HAINTS *let* PEER *go in order to catch her, and, in the tumult and confusion,* PEER *grabs a pistol from one of them, fires it over their heads, and makes good his escape.)*

KING: After him!

HAINTS: Kill him! Kill him! Kill, kill, kill!

(The HAINTS *rush out after* PEER. *The* KING *comforts his daughter.)*

KING: Foolish girl. Now maybe you'll listen to your old pap. Your cousin Grover's not so bad—

WOMAN IN GREEN: Oh, daddy, cousin Grover twitches and drools and drags his knuckles something awful—

KING: I grant ye. Well, what about your second cousin and great-uncle, the Skookumchuck Kid? Now there's a good-lookin' young fella. Both ears bit off in a barroom brawl—

(*The* KING *and the* WOMAN IN GREEN *exit.*)

Scene Seven

(*Pitch dark. We hear* PEER *enter, finding his way through the forest. He stops moving.*)

PEER: Who's there? Someone's there. I can smell you. What are you?

(*A soft, deep, amplified* VOICE *answers.*)

VOICE: I'm me, is all, and no one else. And who are you? Do you know?

PEER: 'Course I do.

VOICE: Then you know more 'n most. You're a lucky man—

PEER: Who are you?

VOICE: I live here. In this night forest. What are you doing here? What do you want?

PEER: I'm lost. I'm far from home.

VOICE: You don't belong here. Go back the way you came.

PEER: No. I can't do that. I'm coming through. Stand aside.

VOICE: There's no coming this way. The shortest distance between two points ain't always a straight line, you know. Sometimes you have to go the long way 'round.

PEER: Who are you, damn you? Show yourself.

VOICE: I'm nobody special. The old man of the forest.

PEER: Old man of the forest. Why, that's what they call Sasquatch.

VOICE: I am he.

PEER: I don't believe you. Sasquatch don't exist. Show yourself.

(PEER *brandishes his pistol.*)

PEER: Show yourself, damn you, I'm coming through—

VOICE: You'd kill me to get where you're going?

PEER: Sure, you get in my way. Same as anyone—

VOICE: Why are you so afraid of me?

PEER: I ain't afraid of you—

VOICE: Yes, you are.

PEER: Well, why shouldn't I be? You ain't human—

VOICE: All the more reason not to be afraid of me.
Go back the way you came. Take the long way 'round—

PEER: Nope. I'm coming through, by God. Stand aside.
Let me by, or I'll—

VOICE: You'll what?

PEER: I'll do what I have to do to get through.

(PEER *rushes forward. An unseen force hurls him back, throws him to the ground.* PEER *points his pistol and fires. The* VOICE *cries out in pain.*)

VOICE: Ah. Stupid boy. Why? Why have you shot me?
You shouldn't've gone and done that. Stupid stupid boy.
You've killed me, sure—

(*Suddenly, torchlight illuminates* PEER, *quivering on the ground. A rush of wind and the* VOICE *disappears. The three* FERAL GIRLS *enter, carrying torches.*)

FIRST FERAL GIRL: Well, lookee here.

SECOND FERAL GIRL: Pretty boy.

THIRD FERAL GIRL: Our lucky day.

PEER: (*Smiles*) Angels. My angels.

FIRST FERAL GIRL: Our pretty boy.

(*They surround him. Something catches the* THIRD FERAL GIRL'*s eye. She holds her torch closer. She exclaims!*)

THIRD FERAL GIRL: Blood! A drop of blood!

(*She reaches down, picks something up, and holds it to the light: a ruby.*)

SECOND FERAL GIRL: A ruby!

FIRST FERAL GIRL: A blood ruby!

THIRD FERAL GIRL: The old man of the forest!

FIRST FERAL GIRL: Pretty boy! What have you gone and done?

(As she turns the stone, a ruby-colored light starts to swirl. They laugh softly and extinguish their torches. Darkness.)

Scene Eight

(Dawn. PEER is discovered, sleeping in a meadow near his home. He wakes, shakes out the cobwebs. Starts. Checks his clothing. The swamp rat rags have disappeared. He's back in his own clothes. He looks around wildly.)

PEER: What?

(Feels his eyes. Looks around. Sees a young girl, ALBERTA, watching him.)

PEER: Hey. Ain't you Sally's sister?

ALBERTA: Yup.

PEER: Alberta. Where am I?

ALBERTA: That's your house yonder, ain't it?

(PEER turns and looks, confused.)

PEER: Yeah. Looks like it. Yeah, I guess it is. How'd I get here? *(Spits)* My mouth tastes like something small and furry took sick in it, lingered some, and then went on ahead and died. Wish I had a stick of candy to suck on. *(To ALBERTA)* You know where Sally is?

ALBERTA: I could find out.

(PEER gropes in his pocket, pulls out a penny, gives it to her.)

PEER: Where is she?

ALBERTA: *(Points)* Hiding over there. Watchin'—

(PEER jumps to his feet. SALLY emerges from hiding.)

PEER: Sally!

SALLY: Don't come any closer. You come any closer, I'll scream—

PEER: What's the matter? You afraid I'll carry you off, too? I'm done with bride-stealing, don't worry. Ain't worth the trouble—

SALLY: Where's Ingrid?

PEER: Where Ingrid is, I couldn't say. We split up.
Some time ago.

SALLY: And you? Where have you been?

PEER: You wouldn't believe me.

SALLY: Try me.

PEER: I met a Haint disguised as a beautiful woman.
She had bright green hair like emeralds. She took me to her
lair. Deep in the middle of the damn Olympic Mountains.
Told me her place was on the very very top of the Big Rock
Candy Mountain—but as a matter of pure fact it turned out
to be smack dab in the middle of some mosquito-infested,
scum-covered, muskrat swamp. Her daddy was a crazy old
coot who called himself King, and wanted to put my eye
out and make me marry her or kill me if I refused, but I
escaped.

SALLY: Oh, Peer. I guess I wouldn't believe you, at that.

(She runs off.)

PEER: Wait! I ain't told you what happened next. Then I run
into Sasquatch—

ALBERTA: What's come over her?

(She starts after SALLY. PEER *grabs her arm.)*

PEER: Wait. Alberta. Give her this.

(He fishes a silver button out of his pocket.)

ALBERTA: What is it?

PEER: What's it look like?

ALBERTA: A button. A silver button.

PEER: Solid silver. Worth a king's ransom. Give it to your
sister. Tell her it's a forget-me-not.

ALBERTA: Forget-me-not.

PEER: Tell her that. Tell her don't forget me—

(PEER lets her go and ALBERTA *disappears. He looks after her.)*

END ACT TWO

ACT THREE

Scene One

(High on a piney ridge. Wet, gray, misty. Cloud country.
PEER *is hacking away at a tree, trying to fell it.)*

PEER: Take that, you old buzzard! And that! Think you're
tough? Not by half, by God! You say your ma was a grizzly
b'ar, 'n your pa was part rattlesnake 'n part gator? You say
you're the meanest sonuvabitch that ever trapped beaver,
hunted buff, panned for gold, fought Indians, sold scalps,
and counted coup in these here mountains, bar none?
Well, I say, the bigger they are the harder they fall!
(He hacks away. The tree falls.) There. What'd I tell you.
Ain't so tough after all. Just whiskey talkin'. Cut you down
to size— *(He sets down his ax.)* Aw, who'm I fooling? Ain't
no mountain man, no Pecos Bill, no Mike Fink, nor Davey
Crockett, neither. Just an old tree, a half-rotted spar, at that.
All this daydreaming and tale spinning. I'm getting too
old for it. Can't afford to lollygag no more. Ain't got my
Ma to look after me now. I'm on my own, every man's
hand dead set against me. Time to put away childish things,
like the Scripture say. I'm an outlaw, truly, a wanted man.
A desperado, and no joke. Nobody to fix my supper, nor
tuck me in at night. Nobody to tell my foolishness to. I
wanna eat now, I got to fend for myself. Wish it were true,
what I told my Ma, that I could do like the grizzlies do,
scoop salmon out of the streams with my bare hands.
Conjure a fire out of a flint. High time to learn, I reckon.
Hope it ain't fixing to rain tonight. Take me some time to
build my palace. One of them San Francisco painted ladies
with all the gingerbread and trimmings! High on Nob Hill!
With all kinds of porches and turrets and balconies and

balustrades! Three storeys, and plenty of curved staircases, and bannisters you can slide down, and mahogany and marble and brass and gilded mirrors and crystal glass throughout! And secret passageways, and rooms full of money, and buried treasure in the back yard— *(He stops for a moment, spits in disgust.)* There I go again. Daydreaming. San Francisco painted palace! I'll be lucky I can get a roof up over my head don't leak so bad I drown. I swear. I can't help myself. I can't keep from daydreaming. My mind is a Fourth-of-July fireworks wheel, spinning and sparking all the time! *(He sets to work trimming the branches from the tree.)* All in my mind. I might think of doing this brave deed, or that, making something of myself, stepping forward where other men cower, face down the bully, save a life, make a fortune, strike it rich, take a gamble, answer the door when opportunity knocks, live large and high on the hog, have a good time and let tomorrow take care of itself, I might dream and scheme about any and all o' that, but only in my mind. But do it? Actually roll up my sleeves and do it? Put my back into it? Nose to the grindstone, and shoulder to the wheel? No, thank you, m'am. Ain't my style. Uh-uh— *(He works on in bitter, silent self-reproach.)*

Scene Two

(A room in HANNAH GYNT's house. Clothes are strewn everywhere. A trunk stands open. HANNAH GYNT and BAD OTTER are going through her things.)

HANNAH GYNT: Bad Otter, remind me. What was I looking for? I swear, I'd forget my head, weren't attached to my neck—

BAD OTTER: Key to the closet.

HANNAH GYNT: That's it. Seen the damn thing?

BAD OTTER: Try the keyhole.

(HANNAH GYNT checks the keyhole.)

HANNAH GYNT: Sure enough. See what I mean? Oh, it's a sin, getting old, a sin, and a shame. What's that sound? The sheriff's wagon, ain't it? Rollin' away—

BAD OTTER: Yup. That's the last one.

HANNAH GYNT: Carrying my poor, worn-out, patched-up
furniture away. Except for my personal effects, and
unmentionables, they've stripped the place.

BAD OTTER: Pret' near.

HANNAH GYNT: Don't seem fair. Punish an innocent old
lady for the deeds of her feckless son. Still and all, I won't
turn my back on Peer. God help me, he's my own flesh and
blood, I can't do other.

BAD OTTER: Stand by him. That's natural.

HANNAH GYNT: There're those who say different. Including
Ingrid Ingersoll's pa. You and your people are kind to take
me in—

BAD OTTER: You have no home—

HANNAH GYNT: It's a right Christian thing to do.

BAD OTTER: *(Protesting)* Please—

HANNAH GYNT: Sorry. I didn't mean no offense. I don't see
why they won't let the whole fandango die down. To try
Peer in absentia like that, find him guilty without a chance
to defend himself, sentence him to hang, and seize my
property, like I was somehow in cahoots with the poor
boy—and all that after Ingrid came strolling back in to
town, pretty as you please, not a mark on her and none
the worse for wear— except in her daddy's eyes, I reckon.
Huh! Little does he know. Butter wouldn't melt in her
mouth, that one. I swear.

(She holds up a shabby, worn, boy's coat.)

HANNAH GYNT: Lookee here. They missed one. I could
patch it up and take it to him. He's prob'ly freezing to
death out there in the mountains.

(She rummages around, comes across a ladle for casting metal.)

HANNAH GYNT: Bad Otter, take a gander. What do you
reckon this is?

BAD OTTER: White folks have many interesting and useless
gadgets.

HANNAH GYNT: This ain't useless. It's for pouring molten
metal, making castings. My late husband, may his soul
rot and burn in hell for all eternity and then some, left this

for Peer. Which is just about all he left him, the sum total except for the bad parts of his character. I blame my husband for the scrape my poor boy's in now, I surely do. The apple don't fall very far from the tree.

BAD OTTER: Nope. Not usually.

HANNAH GYNT: He used to make the boy buttons when he was a baby, tin buttons and tell him they were solid silver. Started right there, you ask me, Peer's confusion about what's real and what ain't.

(She finds a couple of flannel shirts and holds them up.)

HANNAH GYNT: Overlooked these, too. Sheriff's getting careless in his old age. I'll take 'em with me, 'case we find my boy. I know he's cold and sorry out there in that godforsaken wilderness. Sheriff won't like me helping Peer, neither will Ingrid's pa, but they can go to blazes—

BAD OTTER: Time to go.

(He picks up a bag of her things and heads for the door.)

HANNAH GYNT: God bless you, Bad Otter, you're a true Christian gentleman—

(BAD OTTER turns and gives her a ferocious look.)

HANNAH GYNT: I mean that in the best possible sense of the word—

(He turns on his heel and leaves. She follows him out.)

Scene Three

(A platform up in the trees. PEER is constructing a lean-to tree house.)

PEER: A far cry from my San Francisco painted lady. But still. Outa harm's way some. Always wanted to live in the trees. Now here I am. Up away from men who'd do me ill 'n women too. And the Duwamish say you cast a hex around the base of the tree and make a moat to keep the forest spirits out, and gremlins, too. Keep the Haints away. Outa your dreams. I hope that's true. 'Cause they been bothering me something fierce, lately. Got so where I'm

feared to lay down at night and fall asleep. 'Fraid they'll
snatch my soul right out of my body.

*(SALLY enters down below. He hears her approach, leans out,
and they see each other. She starts.)*

SALLY: Oh! Hi.

PEER: Sally?

SALLY: The same.

PEER: What are you doing here?

SALLY: Aint' you glad to see me?

PEER: Sure I am. Sight for sore eyes.

SALLY: I got your message.

PEER: Message?

SALLY: *(Pulls out button)* The silver button you gave Alberta,
to give to me—

PEER: That's what brought you here?

SALLY: Forget me not, you said, didn't you? Well, I ain't
forgot. I been thinking about you. Day and night.

PEER: Me too. About you, I mean.

SALLY: I can't sleep, thinking about you.

PEER: Me neither. Why'd you run away when I come back?

SALLY: Afraid.

PEER: Of me?

SALLY: Afraid of you. Afraid of what my Pa might say.
Mostly, afraid of what I felt in my poor heart. Ever since I
met you, I been all stirred up inside. Forget me not. I tried.
God knows I did. But I can't. I took a chance you'd feel
similar, and here I am. I ain't forgot about you. Have you
forgot about me?

PEER: No, I ain't. Not for a single second.

SALLY: Can I come up, then?

PEER: Oh, yeah. Give you a hand.

(He helps her into the tree. She looks around.)

SALLY: Nice view. Looks like you could see all the way to
China on a clear day—

PEER: Not quite. What about your Pa?

SALLY: I'm quits with him. With my Ma, too. With all my kin. Even little Alberta. I cried like a baby, to leave my folks behind. I've staked everything on this one roll of the dice. That you'd want to be with me, the way I want to be with you.

PEER: I do. I do. We'll get married.

SALLY: You mean it?

PEER: I do, Sally, I do. I swear.

SALLY: Well, that'd be fine by me, Peer.

PEER: I'll never let you down.

SALLY: I believe you.

(They kiss, long and sweet.)

SALLY: Dearest.

PEER: Sweetheart.

SALLY: I feel like I've come home.

PEER: This here house in the trees will be our home. And as long as we're together, we won't have to worry about spirits, and ghosts and goblins, and the Haints of the forest. Nor our human enemies, neither.

SALLY: That's right. They won't hurt us here.

PEER: Sally?

SALLY: Yes, Peer?

PEER: You sure?

SALLY: Sure about what, darling?

PEER: Sure you want to be with me.

SALLY: Yes. It's what I want.

PEER: Be careful what you ask for. You just might get it.

SALLY: What?

PEER: Nothing. There's no going back to the life you knew before. I'm an outlaw, truly.

SALLY: Then I'll be an outlaw's wife.

(They kiss again.)

SALLY: I'm tired from my trip.

PEER: Lay down and rest.

SALLY: Alright.

PEER: Close your eyes and catch some sleep now, and I'll go on and get us some supper.

SALLY: Yes, darling.

(SALLY *lies down and falls asleep.* PEER *slips down out of the tree. Almost immediately he encounters the* WOMAN IN GREEN, *now grown very old, who has an* UGLY BOY *of fourteen with her. The* UGLY BOY *is twisted and misshapen in that Haint sort of way.* PEER *doesn't recognize the* WOMAN IN GREEN *immediately, she's aged so much in such a short time.*)

WOMAN IN GREEN: Hello, Peer Gynt.

PEER: Who're you?

WOMAN IN GREEN: Your neighbors, Peer.

PEER: Ain't no neighbors up here. Not even Indians. And how'd you know my name?

WOMAN IN GREEN: Oh, we're neighbors, alright. And I know your name same way you know mine.

PEER: You're mistaken, m'am. I ain't made your acquaintance heretofore this very moment.

WOMAN IN GREEN: Oh, yes you have. We know each other well. In fact, we're kin, of sorts, though we ain't seen hide nor hair of one another for quite some time—

PEER: I beg to differ. You've got me confused with someone else. Now, if you'll excuse me, I've got chores to do before it's dark—

WOMAN IN GREEN: You made me a promise—

PEER: Me? I think not—

WOMAN IN GREEN: The last time we met.

PEER: We ain't never met, I tell you—

WOMAN IN GREEN: The last time we met was the first time we met—

PEER: Oh, riddles is it? Let's see. So you're saying, if I follow you, we met *once* before. Well, I'm sorry, I don't recollect. Now, I'll be on my way—

WOMAN IN GREEN: You drank a toast with my daddy. You swore an oath—

PEER: You're loco—

WOMAN IN GREEN: Do what you gotta do to get through. You done that yet? Peer?

(PEER *stares, horrified. Now he knows who she is.*)

WOMAN IN GREEN: I guess you have at that, haven't you, Peer? *(Re:* UGLY BOY*)* Well, I have too. *(To* UGLY BOY*)* Your Daddy's hungry. Give him a piece of that bear jerky you been chewing on.

PEER: Daddy! That boy ain't mine. You and me, we never—

WOMAN IN GREEN: Don't say we never. I was there, remember? And it was sweet—

PEER: Just that once—

WOMAN IN GREEN: Once is all it takes, where I come from.

PEER: But that boy's fourteen, if he's a day. And you've aged thirty years, yourself. I hardly recognize you. And all that wasn't more 'n a month ago, at most. This can't be real.

WOMAN IN GREEN: Time rolls up on our kind in a hurry, away from home.

PEER: No! It ain't possible! Anyway, it was all a dream in the first place. It never really happened! I was struck by lightning and had my senses scrambled—

WOMAN IN GREEN: Oh, it happened alright. *(Shoves* UGLY BOY *forward)* Say hey to your pa—

UGLY BOY: Pa!

(*He clings to* PEER's *leg.*)

WOMAN IN GREEN: Chip off the old block, ain't he?

PEER: Get away from me!

(*He scrapes the* UGLY BOY *off and shoves him away. The* UGLY BOY *commences to bawl.*)

UGLY BOY: Ma! He denied me! My pa denied me!

(*The* UGLY BOY *sends up a hellacious howl.*)

PEER: Shut up! Shut your mouth!

WOMAN IN GREEN: You'd deny your own son?

PEER: Ain't my son! Can't be!

WOMAN IN GREEN: He's yours! He's the fruit of your loins. Don't you remember? The time we had—

PEER: Get away from me, you ugly old Haint—

WOMAN IN GREEN: I'm old because you left me. My Daddy
turned me out. I had my baby by myself, in the middle of
the swamp, in the dead of night, under a full moon, with a
pillow made out o' rattlesnakes, and a wolf for a midwife.
And I been searching for you since the night our boy was
born, and the wolf bit through the cord and gobbled up the
afterbirth. I know I'm old and ugly now. But you can make
me young again, Peer Gynt. Like I was. Like I was the night
you enjoyed my favors and said you loved me. Just send
that woman away and make love to me—

PEER: What woman?

WOMAN IN GREEN: What woman? That's rich. Who do you
think you're fooling? The woman you got up there, in that
house in the trees.

PEER: How'd you know that?

WOMAN IN GREEN: This ain't hard for a Haint to know.
'Sides I put a spell on her. Made her lovesick for you.
Followed her here to find you—

PEER: That ain't true. You ain't hexed her. She loves me of
her own accord—

WOMAN IN GREEN: Guess you'll never know that, now.
Guess you'll never be sure.

PEER: Sally! Sally!

WOMAN IN GREEN: She can't hear you. She's in a deep deep
sleep—

PEER: Sally!

(No response. The WOMAN IN GREEN smiles.)

WOMAN IN GREEN: Take me back. Turn her out.

PEER: Never.

WOMAN IN GREEN: I'll be here every day. I'll watch
while the two of you make love. I'll come between you,
whatever you do, I'll be there. You'll never get rid of me.
Or your son—

PEER: Ain't my son—

WOMAN IN GREEN: Oh yes, he is. He's yours, and nobody
else's. Go ahead. Get hitched to that sweet little girl.
You're still my husband, in the eyes of all that's unholy.

UGLY BOY: Hey, Pa. Go ahead and deny us. I'll gut you like a jack rabbit.

WOMAN IN GREEN: *(Kisses him)* Good boy! Pretty boy! Sweet boy! Be just like your daddy when you grow up.

PEER: Go away. Get out of this territory. Go back to your own country, where you belong. I rue the day I ever conjured you up.

WOMAN IN GREEN: I was what you wanted. Now you're stuck with me. It's hard, getting what you desire—

PEER: Poor Sally—

WOMAN IN GREEN: The innocent suffer. It's the way of the world. Come along, son. Kiss your pa good-bye—

UGLY BOY: Weasel! Wolverine! Pissant! Lick-spittle!

(The UGLY BOY spits at PEER and stomps off.)

WOMAN IN GREEN: Pretty boy.

(The WOMAN IN GREEN gives PEER a gummy smile.)

WOMAN IN GREEN: 'Bye for now. Darling.

(She follows the UGLY BOY off.)

PEER: The shortest distance between two points ain't always a straight line, Sasquatch said. Sometimes you have to go the long way 'round. Do what you gotta do to get through. So much for my dream palace in the trees. Thought I'd come home for a minute, there. Thought I'd found my place. Well, can't be helped. What to do? Take the long way around. I can't let Sally get herself mixed up in my troubles. Got myself into this mess. Got to get myself out—

(SALLY awakens, stirs, calls out for PEER.)

SALLY: Peer? Peer? Where are you, darling?

PEER: Down here.

(She looks for him.)

SALLY: There you are. Come up! Come home! Have I been asleep long?

PEER: Not so long.

SALLY: Come up and be with me—

PEER: I still have to find our supper.

SALLY: Don't be long.

PEER: I'll be back soon as I can.

SALLY: Promise?

PEER: Promise. Sally?

SALLY: Yes, dear?

PEER: Be patient. I'll be back.

SALLY: I'll wait for you. I'll be here.

(PEER *nods and leaves.* SALLY *brushes her hair and hums to herself.)*

Scene Four

(BAD OTTER's *camp.* HANNAH GYNT *lies on her sickbed, fretting.)*

HANNAH GYNT: Oh, Lord, let him come. Before You take me home, let me see my boy's face, just one more time. Give me the strength to hang on until he gets here. Oh Lord, where is he? Why don't he come?

(BAD OTTER *enters with* PEER.)

BAD OTTER: Miz Gynt. Peer's here. I brought him down from the side of Mount Shuksan.

(PEER *goes to her side.)*

HANNAH GYNT: Peer.

PEER: Ma.

HANNAH GYNT: You bad boy. Where you been?

PEER: Hiding out.

HANNAH GYNT: That's a wise course of action, when you're a wanted man.

PEER: Why'm I still wanted, Ma? Tell me that. Ingrid came home a long time ago. They still sore 'bout that old folderol? Ain't that commotion calmed down?

HANNAH GYNT: They carry a grudge around these here parts, they surely do. They'll string you up and finish you off on general principles. You ain't safe here.

PEER: I'll be on my way in a minute, Ma. I just came to say goodbye.

HANNAH GYNT: Come close. Let me look at you.

(PEER *leans in. She takes his face in her hands, scrutinizes it.*)

HANNAH GYNT: You've changed.

PEER: Maybe.

HANNAH GYNT: What has happened to you?

PEER: I don't know yet.

HANNAH GYNT: It's hard, being cast out.

PEER: I don't mind. I can take care of myself.

HANNAH GYNT: Can you, Peer? Can you?

PEER: Yes, Ma.

HANNAH GYNT: That's good. I hope so. I ain't got much time.

PEER: What do you mean?

HANNAH GYNT: I'm going home to meet my maker.

PEER: Ain't so, Ma.

HANNAH GYNT: True, son. My last wish is that you'll stay safe, fend for yourself, marry some nice girl and settle down. Peer? Promise me something.

PEER: Yes, Ma.

HANNAH GYNT: Bury me under the willow. Promise me.

PEER: Hush, Ma. Plenty of time to talk about such matters at a later date. Let's talk about something else now. Fill me in. What's happened since I been gone? What's the news? What's the gossip?

HANNAH GYNT: Mostly about poor Sally.

PEER: Poor Sally?

HANNAH GYNT: They say she broke with her mama, and her papa, too, and all her kin. They cried and carried on, but she was resolute and turned her back. And ran off to the mountains to be with some boy, she wouldn't say who. You heard tell anything about her?

PEER: No, m'am. Not a word.

HANNAH GYNT: No idea where she might be?

PEER: No, m'am.

HANNAH GYNT: Some folks say she run off to be with you—

PEER: Sally? Don't be silly, Ma. What would Sally want with the likes of me?

HANNAH GYNT: You tell me, Peer Gynt.

PEER: I don't know nothing about Sally, so help me. Swear.

HANNAH GYNT: Alright, boy. I believe you.

(She groans suddenly, in pain.)

PEER: Ma, what's the matter?

HANNAH GYNT: This bed is hard, and my old joints ache so.

PEER: Ma, you ain't old.

HANNAH GYNT: I've had a hard life, Peer. A hard life, full of sorrow and regret.

PEER: I'm sorry. I know I'm the cause—

HANNAH GYNT: You couldn't help it. It was your nature to be the way you are. Can't change that—

(PEER takes her hand.)

PEER: Ma, remember when we used to tell stories at the fire? Places we'd go when I got rich? See the wide world and all its glories?

HANNAH GYNT: I remember.

PEER: We'll do that. I'll go away and come back for you.

HANNAH GYNT: Oh, Peer—

PEER: I will. 'Course you may not recognize me, at first.

HANNAH GYNT: Not recognize my own son? Why, I'd know you anywhere.

PEER: Well, you won't recognize the silk top hat. Or the shiny shoes. Or the coach and driver. Or the new dress I've got for you. Or the trunkful of fineries, lace and satin. We'll take 'em down to the dock, and get us on board a sailing ship—

HANNAH GYNT: Oh, Peer. That sounds lovely. Where's it bound for?

PEER: China, for starters.

HANNAH GYNT: China! Fancy that!

PEER: We'll sail to China in high style, you and me. And when we get there, we'll have 'em take us directly to the Emperor. The Forbidden City! And we'll pass the time of day with him. And eat candied pheasant, and nightingale tongues, and other such stuff as Chinese Emperors eat.

HANNAH GYNT: China. I've always wanted to see China. Will we be upside down, you reckon?

PEER: I reckon. But so will everybody else, so you won't hardly notice.

HANNAH GYNT: I look forward to it.

(She closes her eyes.)

PEER: And after China, maybe we'll go up Russia way, and pay a call on the Tzar. Eat caviar and drink vodka. I'll buy you furs to keep you warm. And then we'll go on to Paris and Constantinople, see what's doing there. We'll have a grand time, and spend money like it was water. Whatever you want, you just say the word, it's yours—

(He stops, leans over, listens for her breathing, looks up at BAD OTTER.*)*

PEER: She's gone. Damn. What am I gonna do now?

BAD OTTER: What she wanted. She was ready to go. She's traveling now. Beyond.

PEER: Beyond?

BAD OTTER: Beyond where the sun and moon rise and set.

PEER: The happy hunting grounds, you mean?

BAD OTTER: Something like that. Only better.

PEER: Bad Otter. See she's buried under the willow? Maybe make a marker for her grave?

BAD OTTER: It's done. Which way you headed?

PEER: Far away as I can get from here.

(He kisses his mother on the forehead and leaves.)

END ACT THREE

END PART ONE

PART TWO

ACT FOUR

Scene One

(A grove of palm trees along the mighty Amazon River. Near sunset. Tropical light, tropical bird songs, tropical breeze. PEER, now a prosperous, well-dressed gentleman in his mid-forties, wearing a white-linen suit, Panama hat, and gold wire-rimmed glasses, is acting as host to a group of similarly prosperous, well-dressed businessmen: MR COTTON, MONSIEUR DUBOIS, HERR EBERKOPF, LORD WIMBLE, SEÑOR VASQUEZ, and SIGNOR TRESCA. The gentlemen are just finishing a late afternoon picnic. PEER refills several snifters and then holds his own up to the light.)

PEER: Ah! Sunset filtered through a glass of cognac! Now there's happiness! How far I've come! To happiness, gentlemen!

(They all toast.)

ALL: Hear, hear! To happiness!

PEER: If we were meant to be happy, then we should be happy, by God! Without remorse. Without regret. Don't look back, I always say.

MR COTTON: I'll drink to that.

ALL: So will I. Me, too. Splendid idea. Hear, hear!

(They all toast and drink.)

HERR EBERKOPF: Und here's a toast to our splendid host, Peer Gynt! *Prost!*

SEÑOR VASQUEZ: *Salud!*

SIGNOR TRESCA: *Dolce far niente!*

MONSIEUR DUBOIS: *Sante!*

LORD WIMBLE: Cheers!

MR COTTON: Mud in your eye!

(They all toast and drink.)

PEER: Thank you, my friends. Perhaps we should also toast my banker, my lawyer, my chef, and my valet—

HERR EBERKOPF: By all means. Them, too!

ALL: Hear, hear! Them, too!

(They all toast and drink.)

SEÑOR VASQUEZ: Señor Gynt. You have outdone yourself. To arrange such a civilized entertainment here in the middle of the jungle, on the banks of the savage Amazon—

HERR EBERKOPF: Remarkable, truly.

MONSIEUR DUBOIS: I quite agree. Monsieur Gynt, you have that certain *je ne sais quois*—

MR COTTON: A man of the world—

SIGNOR TRESCA: An authentic cosmopolitan—

HERR EBERKOPF: A genuine voluptuary—

LORD WIMBLE: Yes, old man, to borrow a term from my froggy friend here—however do you come by your *savoir faire*?

(PEER cuts a cigar, lights it, and smokes it with great pleasure, as he talks.)

PEER: Gentlemen, I ask you. What should a man be? What should he hope to be? What should he want to be? The answer to all these questions is easy: himself. He should be himself.

MR COTTON: Easier said than done, my friend.

PEER: No question. But I've managed it. I've always come out on top. By my wits and nerves. And by, I must admit, virtue of never having married. The hell, you say. No. This—choice—was essential. To be so unburdened with the responsibility for another, so unaffected by another's moods—I count myself a lucky man indeed. Not to mention children. The terrifying pitter-patter of little feet. Of course, I almost married once. But fortunately, it was

married once. But fortunately, it was not to be. And how
could I, of all men, have a home? A domestic life. Civic
duties. I am a citizen of the wide world. A globetrotter,
they call it. Well, just so. How far I've come. Still and all,
I might easily have ended up a petty clerk in some dismal
backwater burg, working in a bank or general store,
keeping accounts for a crummy, small-town tyrant. If I'd
married. If I hadn't left home to see the world when I did.
There was something of a rush to tie the knot, if you know
what I mean. Fortunately for me, the difficulties with her
family were simply insurmountable. I just couldn't agree
to her father's conditions, his stipulations. He wanted me
to renounce everything that made me me. My Gyntish
nature, so to speak. So I turned my back on a kind of life
others yearn for. A potential fortune, a secure hearth and
homestead, heirs. Sacrificed to self-discovery. And I'll tell
you something else. I had to fight her seven brothers to do
it.

ALL: Seven brothers! My goodness!

PEER: Bloodshed ensued. Say no more. I have no regrets.
None. What's done is done. All in all, things have worked
out better than I could ever have imagined. I've come
a long way from the old homestead. Am I happy? Yes.
I would have to say, without a moment's hesitation,
I am happy, yes I am.

(He tastes his drink, puffs on his cigar.)

PEER: What's meant to be will be.

SEÑOR VASQUEZ: *Que sera, sera.*

PEER: Couldn't have put it better myself, Señor Vasquez.
Destiny.

HERR EBERKOPF: You have a comprehensive world view,
my friend. Und yet you say you have never been to college?

PEER: I have gaps, I grant you. I am self-taught. I know
a little about most things, a lot about some. Commerce.
I know trade. I have sailed the mercantile seas and
prospered. I know Philosophy. History. Bits and pieces
about the places I've been. I've taught myself how to speak
properly. Grammar. I almost never say 'ain't' no more.
A small joke. How to dress. Which fork to use. Of course,

I've always read, whatever I could get my hands on, and
that's been a great help to me over the years. I started out
without a nickel to my name, after all. Left home, worked
my way down the Coast. Whatever I could find. Logger,
cook, stevedore. It was my great good luck to arrive in
California at precisely the right historical moment. The
gold rush was only just beginning when I disembarked in
San Francisco. Men were coming down out of the hills with
nuggets the size of your fist. If you were lucky and smart,
knew where to look and how to keep what you found,
you could make your fortune in a matter of weeks. Of
course, most men are neither lucky nor smart.

ALL: Luck nor smart, too true.

PEER: Many's the man who went up in those hills to look
for gold and ended up broke or dead, or both.

LORD WIMBLE: You have to be lucky *and* smart to prosper in
this world.

PEER: I was both. The fever dream of gold that infected
other men left me cold. It was clear to me there was another
sort of fortune to be made.

SIGNOR TRESCA: Please enlighten us, Signor Gynt. What on
earth is better than gold?

PEER: Grubstake.

HERR EBERKOPF: Grubstake?

SEÑOR VASQUEZ: Que es grubstake?

PEER: Rope and mules, pans and sieves for sifting gravel,
shovels and picks for moving earth, and coffee and
flour and sugar and beans. Canvas for tents. Guns and
ammunition. Which is where I first learned a thing or two
about weapons. And whiskey. Whiskey most of all. I sold
prodigious amounts of whiskey. Oceans of it. And women,
too, I must admit. Every whore in North America was
drawn to the gold rush, like grizzly bears to a salmon
stream in spawning season, and I put plenty to work.
What the hell. The lucky and smart ones became rich and
opened their own houses. And I became rich, too. Richer
than any miner or madam. And then the veins played out,
the rush died down, the miners and harlots moved on to
Nevada, and I bought boats and got into the China trade.

Interesting business, the China trade. I moved most
anything to and from those heathen shores. Ivory. Jade.
Sapphires. Opium. Rhinocerous horn, for God's sake.

MR COTTON: At a prodigious profit, I presume.

PEER: I made a fortune. Took 'em guns and whiskey,
brought coolies back.

ALL: Coolies! My, my. Really. How unusual. How—

PEER: Supply and demand, gentlemen. They needed
Chinamen to build the railroad east. Back east, they were
using the Irish, to build the railroad west, but I couldn't
get Irishmen. So I got Chinamen. Didn't make me the most
popular fellow in San Francisco, I grant you, I could not
have run for mayor, but somebody had to do it. Brought
coolies over by the shipload. Thousands of them.

MR COTTON: But the coolie trade, my friend. Didn't it keep
you awake nights?

PEER: Not at all. Chinese coolies, Irish, what's the
difference? They *wanted* to come. Couldn't wait to get here.
The Promised Land. Gold Mountain, they called it. They
planted poppies along the railroad tracks to mark their
passage. See 'em all over the West, blooming in the spring.
I always wondered about that moment. When the railroads
were joined, spanning the continent. When the Chinese,
working their way east, met the Irish, working their way
west. Somewhere in Nebraska. Did they shake hands?
Pose for a group portrait? Most likely they just stared at
one another. Who the hell are you, and how the hell did
you get *here*? And what the hell are you going to do now?
That would have been something to see. Anyway, in time
I grew tired of the China trade and in my wanderlust
longed for new bazaars. I then discovered that I could go
anywhere in the world and sell guns. Man's appetite for
weaponry is insatiable. And why not? The world is a hard
place. Blood is currency freely traded, and life is cheap.
Men are perfectly willing to kill to get what they want, and
they need only the wherewithal to do so. *Voila.* Enter your
obliging arms merchant, the man who can make your
bloodiest dreams come true.

MONSIEUR DUBOIS: Nothing wrong with the arms trade—

ALL: No, no, the arms trade, nothing at all—

LORD WIMBLE: I have dabbled a bit in cannon myself—

PEER: Let the Little Sisters of the Poor beat their breast and tear their hair all they want, I make no apologies. Those who say I have blood on my hands should look to their own. Who among us has not dreamed of murder? Of recourse to violence? Of settling a debt, avenging a wrong, or ridding oneself of a tormentor? I submit that those who have avoided bloodshed have more likely done so from cowardice than scruple, from fear of retribution than because they could not stomach violence. Aversion to violence is not natural. It goes against the human grain, does it not? You compliment me on being civilized, and I thank you, but it's an acquired taste, the civilized life. Don't you agree?

MR COTTON: One hundred and ten percent.

LORD WIMBLE: A thin veneer, civilization.

MONSIEUR DUBOIS: C'est vrai. Beneath the surface, chaos lurks. Only the bulwark of the bourgeoisie holds back the forces of anarchy.

PEER: I quite agree. Anyway, to balance my, some would say, unholy trade, and since you never know when the Almighty will decide to cash you out and count your chips and markers, I loaded my boats with missionaries, to go along with my guns. All denominations, without preference. I saw a certain symmetry in this arrangement. If lives were taken by those using my wares, I thought I might square accounts, if indeed they needed squaring, by saving souls. And I've reckoned, over the years, that the missionaries I transported to various and sundry distant shores baptized as many heathens as ever perished at the muzzles of the guns they bought from me. The give and take of the world is a marvelous thing, don't you think? The Chinese call it the yin and yang. Take a life, save a soul.

HERR EBERKOPF: I see you have worked things out very neatly, Herr Gynt.

PEER: Well, Herr Eberkopf, in accounting, as you know, for every debit there is a credit, and it all zeroes out in the end. Plus, the missionary traffic proved surprisingly profitable.

Of course, I was just servicing a need, and if I hadn't
done it, there were plenty of enterprising young fellows
clamoring to take my place. My career as an arms merchant
reached its zenith during our recent Civil War. I ran guns
to both sides. I bought my way through the Federal
blockade by selling them copies of my manifests, lists of
precisely what weapons I was running to the Rebs. I then
in turn sold the Confederates the exact locations and
descriptions of the Union vessels. Worked out well for
everyone. A man in my position often has saleable
information as well as hard goods to offer to the highest
bidder. Some may call it espionage. I call it opportunity,
and the obligation of every citizen of the world.

ALL: Hear, hear, quite agree, no question about it,
obligation, just so, citizen of the world, nothing more.

PEER: But I must confess, the gun trade has started to bore
me, and I can't deny there is an inherent grubbiness to the
entire enterprise which eventually rubs off over the years,
working its way into the fabric of one's life like a fine soot.
I'm getting on, after all, and I want to be received at last
in polite society without that almost indiscernable curl
of the lip I invariably encounter whenever my profession
is revealed. That slight chill that wafts through the room
like a sudden unwelcome breeze from a sewer, and then
subsides as civilized conversation resumes. There is a
particular stench of moral superiority that can really put
you off your feed. It has me, on many occasions.

HERR EBERKOPF: I know what you mean.

MONSIEUR DUBOIS: *Moi, aussi.*

SEÑOR VASQUEZ: Let's face it, they hate us.

LORD WIMBLE: Yes, the upper crust look down their
noses at chaps like us. Don't want to get their hands dirty,
do they? Old money. Think they came by it honestly,
somehow. As if it was given to them in the Garden of Eden,
and they're entitled to it for all eternity.

(PEER *puffs contemplatively, and shrugs.*)

PEER: We so-called robber barons will ultimately be granted
our place in polite society. All will be forgiven, in time.
Philanthropy. Largesse. A museum here, a university there,

a park, a hospital. People will revise their opinions of us.
Once reviled, we'll be revered. All in good time. I'm not
quite ready yet to part with my fortune. Time enough for
that when I'm old and respectable. Which is what brought
me at last to Mexico. The quest for a more respectable
line of work. I bought a silver mine. I own the mine, the
railroad which takes the ore to the coast, the smelter which
refines it, and the ships which transport the finished ingots
to the States.

SIGNOR TRESCA: A rather neat monopoly, Mr Gynt.

PEER: Did I mention the miners? I own them, too.
And the company store. What could be more respectable?

SEÑOR VASQUEZ: Where in Mexico, Senor Gynt?

(PEER *takes a drink. He is getting a little tipsy.*)

PEER: Taxco. Charming town. Spanish colonial architecture.
Cobblestone streets. Mountain air. And the women. Well.
It's true what they say. The farther south you go, the
warmer it gets.

ALL: It's true, it's true, the farther south, the warmer they
get.

MR COTTON: Very interesting, sir, but what I want to know
is—you've brought us here to the ends of the earth for a
purpose, haven't you? When do we get started? Where are
the damn diamonds?

ALL: Yes, the diamonds, where are they? Let's get started.

PEER: Gentlemen. Just upriver is what we're looking for.
Diamonds the size of Easter eggs. Acres of them! Just
waiting to be gathered up by the bushel basket!

(PEER *takes a velvet drawstring bag out of his pocket, opens it
and spills the contents: a small fortune in diamonds.*)

MONSIEUR DUBOIS: *Mon dieu!*

MR COTTON: Are they real?

PEER: Real as the day is long. Gentlemen. Our destiny
awaits us.

ALL: Diamonds! Diamonds! Diamonds!

PEER: Yes, indeed! We'll be rich!

MONSIEUR DUBOIS: We're already rich.

PEER: We'll be richer!

ALL: Hear, hear! Richer! Richer! Richer!

(They all drink and toast.)

HERR EBERKOPF: Tell me, Herr Gynt. Why are *you* interested in this venture? Surely you have enough money—

PEER: It's not the money, God knows. I have enough money to live like a king for the rest of my life. But what would I do? Who would I be if I didn't pursue my business interests? My Gyntish nature? I wouldn't be Peer Gynt, would I? Let them call me robber baron. I'll be Peer Gynt, Robber Baron. Sir Peer, to you, and show some respect. And besides. I don't yet have enough money to do what I want. A man can do well for himself in a place like this. Make himself a king. Not literally of course. That's the mistake the nitwit Frenchman made, no offense, Monsieur DuBois, what's his name, Maximillian the Third, or some such nonsense. You can call yourself Emperor of Mexico, but they'll put you up against a wall and shoot you just the same. Or you can be Emperor of Mexico, quietly, in all but name.

HERR EBERKOPF: Or the Amazon.

PEER: Yes. Emperor of the Amazon. Indeed. *(Smiles)* These countries are in turmoil. Chaos. Revolution brewing. Oh, yes, a man can do very well in a place like this. The sky's the limit. Money is power, gentlemen. And, truth be told, you can never have enough money, or enough power. Never enough. Which is why we formed our little consortium, and why I've brought you here, to this savage wilderness. I mean to be Emperor of the Amazon. And the Andes. And Mexico. From the Rio Grande to Tierra Del Fuego! The fulfillment of my Gyntish nature!

LORD WIMBLE: My dear boy, aren't Emperors out of style?

PEER: Brazil has one. Dom Pedro the Second. I'll be Peer the First!

MR COTTON: That reminds me. We're in Brazil at this moment, are we not?

PEER: It won't be called Brazil for long. I think I'll name this part of my Empire—Peeruvia.

(They laugh. PEER drains his drink and smacks his lips.)

PEER: The firing squad used my bullets and my guns to cut the French adventurer and his hysterical wife down to size. I derive a great deal of satisfaction from that fact. Now, if you'll excuse me, gentlemen—all this brandy and good food and civilized conversation has made me sleepy. I'm going to retire for a brief nap in yonder hammock, and then we'll return to the boat, for an evening of cards and fine cigars.

(He strolls off. The six robber barons gather around, looking at the gems.)

MR COTTON: The man's mad!

HERR EBERKOPF: Emperor of the Amazon!

LORD WIMBLE: Peeruvia!

SEÑOR VASQUEZ: And we are to be his court jesters, I suppose.

SIGNOR TRESCA: Nothing crazy about these gems. *Bella! Bellissima!*

MONSIEUR DUBOIS: No, no. The diamonds are quite rational. On this point, he's not deluded. There's a fortune here.

SEÑOR VASQUEZ: Once we get back to civilization, such a man will find a way to cheat his partners out of what he owes them, mark my words.

MR COTTON: Grind us under his heel.

LORD WIMBLE: Quite right. Can't trust him. Completely unscrupulous.

MR COTTON: What are you talking about? We won't ever get back to civilization.

HERR EBERKOPF: *Ja.* He'll leave us to die in this godforsaken wilderness.

MONSIEUR DUBOIS: He'll slit our throats in our sleep.

SEÑOR VASQUEZ: What will we do?

MR COTTON: Do unto others before they do unto you. I'm sure the crew can be bribed. If not—

(He draws a gun.)

MR COTTON: There are other means of persuasion. Let's go.

SIGNOR TRESCA: Which way to the diamond fields?

Señor Vasquez: Upriver, he said.

Monsieur Dubois: *Allons!*

Herr Eberkopf: What about Herr Gynt?

Signor Tresca: Shall we kill him now?

Mr Cotton: Leave him for the crocs and skeeters.

(They steal away, taking the diamonds with them.)

Scene Two

(Peer is running along the river bank, chasing after his stolen yacht. He's distraught, wild. It is night, and the jungle is dark and scary.)

Peer: No! It can't be! Come back! This is a nightmare! I'll wake up in a minute! My God! Traitors! Thieves! Come back! *(He looks to Heaven.)* Oh, Lord! Bring them back! Stop them! If You won't stop them, make them pay! Punish them! Wreck them! Strand them in the jungle and leave them to die, as they've left me! Deliver them to the mercy of the hostile natives! Give them blackwater fever and malaria! Feed them to the piranhas! *(He stops, catches his breath.)* No. There they go. They're sailing out of sight, quite happily. They'll come back after the crocodiles have picked my carcass clean and harvest the diamonds. Drink champagne over my bones. They'll be rich, and I'll be dead, thank you very much. Clearly God has not heard my curses. Well, why would He, and how could He, in this godforsaken place? We are far from God, here. Far, far, far from God. Perhaps if I got down on my knees. *(He gets down on his knees, looks to Heaven, and prays.)* Oh, Lord. I'm getting out of the arms racket, I promise You, once and for all. And I quit the coolie trade some time back, if You recall. And I did send those missionaries to China, although, Lord, if You'd gotten a good look at some of those folks, You might count that against me, but I was doing what I thought You'd like. Sure, if You think about it, I'm due a little good fortune, here. If You'll just wreck those rascals on the nearest rapids, I'd be ever so grateful. And maybe You could arrange to have them fall into the tender

clutches of some local headhunters, while You're at it.
I don't think that's asking too much, I really don't.

(There is a sudden huge explosion, a flash of light. PEER scrambles to his feet and looks downriver.)

PEER: Oh, my God. He heard me after all. They're wrecked!
They're done for! Just what they deserve, those bastards!
What luck! *(He is suddenly moved to tears.)* No. More than
mere luck. You're looking after me, aren't You? As You
always have. To survive while all the others perish, that's
something more than luck. You keep Your eye on me, don't
You? Despite my faults and failings. Yes, indeed. What a
wonderful feeling! I feel blessed! Truly.

(A jaguar roars. PEER jumps.)

PEER: Oh my God. What was that? A lion? They don't have
lions in Brazil. A jaguar. A very hungry jaguar. Hunting for
its dinner, no doubt. Oh, my God. I'm going to die. If I
don't get eaten by a jaguar, a python'll wrap itself around
me while I'm sleeping and squeeze the stuffing out of me.
And what am I going to do for food? If I weren't so scared,
I'd be famished. *(He slaps at mosquitoes.)* Luck, eh? Slow
torture is more like it. They're eating me alive, the little
bastards. Pretty soon, I'll wish I'd been on that boat when
it went up in flames. Put me out of my misery. Where am
I going to spend the night? In a palm tree, that's it. Can
jaguars climb trees? I'm sure they can. And so can snakes.
Well, there's nothing else to do. There's one. Tall, with a
big bushy frond to hide in. *(He climbs up in a palm tree and
arranges himself.)* There. That's better. Some. At least I have
a fighting chance. Lord? I take back what I said a minute
ago. I know You're looking after me. I'm glad to be alive,
no matter what. That jaguar gave me a scare, that's all.
Took me by surprise.

*(There's a rustle in the trees. PEER freezes. He leans over and
parts the fronds. Starts. Staring at him is an APE, who hoots and
screeches. PEER is so startled, he falls out of the tree, and lands
with a thud.)*

PEER: Ouch! Damn! I've busted my tailbone, God damnit!
Sorry, Lord. But it hurts.

*(He pulls himself to his feet and screams and yells and waves his
arms at the APE.)*

PEER: Hey, you! Go away! Monkey face! Out of my palm tree, you great ape!

(The APE *just hoots and hollers back.* PEER *picks up a stone and throws it. He's met with a hail of rocks in return.)*

PEER: Oh, my God! Look out! Ouch! Damn that smarts! Ouch! He's trying to kill me!

*(*PEER *retreats. The* APE *beats its breast, victorious.* PEER *picks up and hurls one last rock.)*

PEER: Take that, you beast!

(He scuttles out under a shower of stones.)

Scene Three

(Morning. PEER *is wandering through the jungle. He's carrying a flute that he's carved from a bamboo cane, and he toots on it, happily. He takes a deep breath, stretches, and sighs.)*

PEER: Ah, this is the life! Fresh air and flowers! And plenty of fruit for the picking! The stench of the city in my nostrils is almost gone! I can't imagine ever going back. I feel free. Master of my own fate, without obligation. Why, I'm Emperor here, of all I survey. My little kingdom. Smell that perfume. My, my. I never would have guessed the jungle was so fragrant! Intoxicating.

(He sits down and plays his flute. Behind him, a shy young AMAZON INDIAN GIRL *appears, drawn by the sound of his flute. She listens as he plays until finally he senses her presence. He turns, sees her, and stops.)*

PEER: Hello.

(He scrambles to his feet. She darts behind a tree. He follows her. He can't find her.)

PEER: Hello? Where'd you go? I won't hurt you.

(He plays. Out of the forest steps the GIRL.*)*

PEER: Ah, there you are.

(Behind her appears an AMAZON INDIAN WARRIOR, *his face brilliantly painted.* PEER's *smile fades. They stare at each other a long moment. Finally:)*

PEER: Pleased to make your acquaintance, I'm sure.

(The WARRIOR gestures with his bow and arrow for PEER to follow them. PEER shrugs.)

PEER: Out of the frying pan, into the fire.

(They go out.)

Scene Four

(Twilight. PEER, dressed in casual, tropical cotton clothes, barefoot, is standing on the ornate, wrought-iron balcony of a hotel room in Lima, Peru. He's drinking rum from a bottle, smoking a cigar, while a beautiful young Peruvian woman, REMEDIOS, sits on the edge of the bed and plays a guitar, softly. PEER looks like he's "gone native" in his appearance and demeanor. He's much less the starchy businessman, and much more the reckless adventurer, the ex-pat freebooter.)

PEER: Remedios. You look radiant this evening.

REMEDIOS: Thank you, *mi amor.*

PEER: Are you going to sing for me this evening?

REMEDIOS: Of course.

(She plays and sings a sad Andean song. It's quite beautiful, and her voice is lovely. When she's done, PEER applauds softly.)

PEER: Lovely. Just lovely. Translate, please.

REMEDIOS: It is a song about how a wealthy stranger appears from a far-off land, and how someday he will return to his home, but for the moment they are happy, the rich man and the poor girl from the Andes.

PEER: Love is fleeting.

REMEDIOS: Yes. Just so. We have a saying: "Love makes time pass. Time makes love pass".

PEER: Ah. I like that saying. And "paloma"? What is "paloma"?

REMEDIOS: Pigeon. Or dove.

PEER: You are my pretty paloma.

(He kisses her.)

REMEDIOS: No. You are mine.

PEER: Lovely Remedios! You make me feel like a boy again. Here.

(He goes to a drawer, opens it, and produces two blue velvet bags with drawstrings. He opens one and spills out a small fortune in diamonds. He holds a few of the gems up to the light. He plucks a diamond from the pile on the bed and hands it to her.)

REMEDIOS: Oh, my goodness! For me? Is it valuable?

PEER: Indeed. You could buy your entire village for half of what that stone is worth.

REMEDIOS: I can't—

PEER: Don't be silly. Take it. It's just a trinket to me. A bauble. Nothing more than trash. If it makes you happy—

REMEDIOS: Oh, yes, my darling—

PEER: Then take it. Take another, while you're at it.

REMEDIOS: Are you certain?

PEER: Any one you please.

(REMEDIOS looks over the diamonds for a moment, and PEER turns his head. REMEDIOS slips a handful of stones into her blouse, and then holds up a second diamond.)

REMEDIOS: I'll take this one. It matches the first.

PEER: You're welcome to it.

(They kiss.)

REMEDIOS: You are too good to me, darling.

PEER: Perhaps.

REMEDIOS: *Mi amor.*

(They kiss again. PEER scoops up the diamonds, puts them back in the bag, and returns the bag to the drawer.)

PEER: Now, where was I in my reminiscence of my season in the Amazon? Have I spoken of it before?

REMEDIOS: Tell me again. You were near death.

PEER: Near death, yes. Abandoned by my erstwhile partners. Wandering through the jungle. Hiding from hostile natives, who appeared suddenly on the river in their dugout canoes, daubed in warpaint, brandishing their blowguns and curare-tipped darts, which they used to murderous effect on the parrots and macaws, shooting scores of them out of the trees for their brilliant plumage.

(He swigs his rum.)

PEER: I staggered on, downstream, half-dead from starvation and sickness. I remember, in my fever, a particular phrase kept running through my brain like a Hindustani mantra: do what you have to do to get through. But I could not recall the source of that phrase, nor can I to this day. Perhaps it's in the Scriptures. More likely I heard it in China. Confucius? Mencius? No matter.

REMEDIOS: And what became of your bad partners, *mi amor*?

PEER: Some days later, I couldn't say how many, for I was half out of my mind with fever, I came across the remains of my yacht. I assumed my betrayers had come to grief upon a particularly treacherous stretch of rapids. And so they had, I was to learn later. But by some stroke of perverse luck, they had survived the rapids and the rocks, only to be captured by headhunters. God had heard my prayers, after all.

(He opens the second velvet bag, pulls out a string of half a dozen shrunken heads. REMEDIOS gasps.)

PEER: My erstwhile partners. May I introduce Mr Cotton, Connecticut Yankee, a banker; Monsieur DuBois from Marseilles, also a banker; Herr Eberkopf of Hamburg, a steel magnate; Lord Wimble, a textile baron from Manchester; and last, but not least, Señor Vasquez, railroads and olives, late of Madrid; and Signor Tresca, who corked an acceptable if overpriced chianti in Tuscany. How nice to see you again, gentlemen. Cost me a pretty penny to acquire these little souvenirs, by the way. The old chief was very attached to them.

REMEDIOS: They are horrible.

PEER: Ah yes. Aren't they just? Anyway, my strength gave out at the last and I collapsed. I was done for, ready for last rites, when I was discovered by a tribe of hostile Indians, who took me as a captive to their village deep in the bush.

REMEDIOS: You said before the Indians were peaceful and shy and nursed you back to health.

PEER: *Au contraire*. They were savage and warlike, and kept me as a slave. And it was only after I had demonstrated my prowess as a shaman that I rose in their estimation, and they made me their medicine man and feared and revered me.

REMEDIOS: I'm certain you said they were gentle people.

PEER: Not at all. In fact, they were the very savages who set upon my treacherous colleagues and took their heads for trophies. What's more, when I regained my senses, I found myself bound hand and foot, about to be plopped into a vat of boiling stew, and the chief standing over me, brandishing for my edification his grisly souvenirs— which were so freshly gotten, they were still dripping wet— and threatening me with an even more gruesome fate.

REMEDIOS: *Mi amor,* I am sure you told me the cannibal headhunters were another tribe—

PEER: Did I? Ah, well. Perhaps I did.

REMEDIOS: And the gentle Indians who rescued you treated you like a god—

PEER: So they did. Like a god. After I brought the youngest daughter of the chief, who was suffering from a mysterious malady, back from the brink of death, they worshipped the very ground I walked on.

REMEDIOS: And you told me it was only recently, years later, that you came across the heads of your friends, in a theatre—

PEER: In the Opera House, at Manaus. By this time the old chief was the last of his tribe. Reduced to hawking his keepsakes in the lobby. Of course, I recognized the craven countenances of my compatriots immediately. We haggled over the price a bit, and I finally gave the old savage a bottle of rum and sixty cruzeiros for all six shrunken heads. Quite a bargain, in my estimation. I would have given a hundred times that amount to own those horrible artifacts. But you're right, dearest. I am a little hazy on the details. It was all a long time ago. You don't doubt me, do you?

REMEDIOS: Not a word.

PEER: What is true, what I know for a fact and remember as if it were yesterday, is that the chief of the tribe, headhunter or no, offered me, after I saved her life, his youngest daughter as a bride.

REMEDIOS: So you've said. But you never answer me when
I ask you: did you take her? When he offered her, did you
accept?

(PEER *smiles mysteriously and puffs on his cigar.*)

PEER: Do you care?

REMEDIOS: No. I don't give a damn.

PEER: I'll tell you then. Since you're not jealous.

REMEDIOS: Go ahead. I don't care.

PEER: The truth is, how could I refuse? I could not.
To decline such a gift? A mortal insult. By the custom of
the country, the old chief would have had to kill me for
insulting his daughter. And her, too, for being shamed.
So I accepted, with thanks. And then we drank many toasts
with the local beer, a foul brew made from fermenting a
root that the Indians chewed up and spat back out. A far
cry from a good Scandinavian lager, I can tell you that.

REMEDIOS: Did you sleep with her?

PEER: Yes. Several times.

REMEDIOS: Was she pretty?

PEER: Pretty enough. Truth be told, scarcely more than a
child. A slip of a thing. Came up to here on me. Barely of
age. Rosebuds for breasts. Long black hair, and large black
liquid eyes. Like yours, my dear.

REMEDIOS: I remind you of her?

PEER: Not in the slightest. I scarcely remember her. It was,
after all, a very long time ago.

REMEDIOS: What happened to her?

PEER: I have no idea. Shortly after the wedding festivities
I slipped away, stole a canoe, and sailed downstream to
the nearest civilized settlement. When I returned to the
diamond fields a year later, the tribe was gone, scattered
to the four winds. And frankly, I never gave them, or her,
a second thought in the intervening years. Until that night
at the Opera House, when I saw the old man, sitting on his
blanket, his ghastly wares spread before him like so many
rotten pieces of fruit.

REMEDIOS: And her father? He didn't tell you? What
happened to her?

PEER: He failed to recognize me as his former son-in-law. It seemed pointless to remind him. *La Boheme*. That's what they were playing that evening. I wasn't in love with her. In case you're curious.

REMEDIOS: Are you in love with me?

PEER: Of course. Madly. Are you in love with me?

REMEDIOS: Until my dying day.

(They kiss. REMEDIOS *slips off her dress,* PEER *takes off his shirt and shoes. They lie down on the bed. The lights dim. Time passes. Love makes time pass.* SALLY *appears on the balcony, now a middle-aged woman, still strong and attractive.)*

SALLY: I'm still here. I'm still waiting for you, Peer. You said you'd return, and I believe you. I sometimes wonder if I'll know you, it's been so long. I often imagine a man will come one day to the door, and I'll ask him if he's you, and he'll say, yes, of course, who do you think, and I'll take him in. I'll take him to my bed. We'll make a life. But he'll be strange to me. And he won't remember certain things. He'll claim to have forgotten everything he ever knew about the town and the people who lived there. He'll have put the past beyond recalling. And the thought will cross my mind he's not you. Not you at all. Not even of this country. A stranger. A wanderer. A man who lost his old life, and went looking for a new one, and took yours. The one I was saving for you. *(Beat)* But I don't believe that will happen. I believe you'll come back. I believe I'll know you for yourself, when you return.

*(*SALLY *disappears, the light on the balcony goes out.* REMEDIOS *gets up quietly, checks to make certain* PEER *is asleep, slips on her dress, goes to the drawer where* PEER *has left the bag of diamonds, opens it, puts the bag down the front of her dress, and slips quietly out of the room.* PEER *leaps up, turns on the light, goes to the drawer, opens it.)*

PEER: Ah ha! She took the diamonds. The bitch. What do you think of that? Ah, well. It wouldn't have lasted. All this lovemaking, I'm getting too old for it. Left her guitar, I see. *(He picks it up, plays a few notes.)* Smart girl. She knew what to take and what to leave behind. Wait! She didn't, perchance, filch the wrong bag by mistake? *(He opens the drawer, takes out the other velvet bag, reaches inside and pulls*

out the string of heads.) No, thank God. She left me my
pretties. Far more precious than diamonds, which are, let's
face it, a dime a dozen, if you know where to look. Let her
choke on them for all I care. But these! These are priceless!
I suppose she lied when she said she loved me. Women.
All but one. Strange. I dreamed of her again tonight. Sally.
*(He pads over in his bare feet, takes a swig from the bottle of
rum.)* She was much too young for me, in any case. I
thought I could teach her something of the world. But,
as you can see, her instincts are rather good. If somewhat
crude. Perhaps she'll use those stones to make something
of herself. Seize her opportunity. She owes me much.
Ungrateful child. *(He contemplates his bottle.)* What is more
foolish, more pathetic, than a mature man and a much
younger woman? He prances and capers, tries to rut
like the young buck he fancies he once was so long ago,
and ends sweating and ruddy, huffing and puffing, red
in the face, and soft where it counts. Of course, I have seen
older women in the south of France paying plenty for the
caresses of pretty boys, so perhaps it is more a question of
wherewithal than anything else. If you have money, you
can purchase certain pleasures, even youth. Even love, or at
least, the illusion of love. If you're poor, you're stuck—you
play the hand that's dealt you. As do we all, in the end,
I suppose. *(He extracts another cigar and smells it
appreciatively.)* Cuban. My own tobacco. My fields,
my factory. I have cane fields in Cuba, too. Sugar mills.
Company stores. Ships. A rum distillery. A cooperage
and a bottler. From start to finish, from sugar cane to your
local bar, every step of the way. Mine. I could inventory
my holdings worldwide for you, but that would be
ostentatious, don't you think? And a bit of a bore. Ah!
Excellent good cigar! *(He lights it and puffs happily.)*
Delicious. Subsequent to my harrowing adventures in the
Amazon and my amorous misadventures in Lima, I
journeyed to Cuzco, the stone city of the Incas. And from
there, to the ruins of Machu Picchu, high in the Andes.
Quite the opposite of the jungle, in every regard. Bitter
cold, and the air diamond bright, and thin. I did as the
Indians do, chewed the leaf of the coca plant, to stave
off the cold, and the dizziness that comes from altitude

sickness. It produces a pleasant, numbing sensation.
Case you didn't know.

(The lights fade.)

Scene Five

*(Night. A tent at an archeological dig high in the Andes, near the
ruins of Machu Picchu. A camp table, some chairs, etc. PEER is
examining some recently excavated artifacts by lantern light.)*

PEER: Ah! Exquisite! Really! First rate. I have an abiding
interest in antiquities and artifacts. As a sideline, I have
been traveling the world, trading in Egyptian, Celtic,
African, Chinese, and pre-Columbian artifacts, to name a
few. The inexorable march of progress across the globe has
unearthed a flood of these objects, and my fellow robber
barons are avid collectors. As are the great museums, the
national galleries of the colonial powers, etcetera. Anyway,
I've struck a deal with the leader of this expedition, and
he's graciously agreed to give me the opportunity to
examine whatever he finds, before he notifies his sponsors
back home in Germany. For a price, of course. Herr Doktor
Bieldfeldt. Good man. First-rate archeologist. He's dug up
some really remarkable stuff. Pottery, jewelry, statuary.
Top-dollar items. If I can't peddle this stuff in New York
City for a pretty profit, my name's not Peer Gynt! Ah!
I hear the good doctor's gentle tred now.

(HERR DOKTOR BIELDFELDT pokes his head in the tent.)

BIELDFELDT: Herr Gynt.

PEER: Herr Doktor. Good evening.

BIELDFELDT: Good evening, Herr Gynt. Is now a good time?

PEER: Never better. Come in, come in.

*(BIELDFELDT comes in. He's middle-aged, sweaty, dirty from
working in the archeological trenches, and nervous. He's got a
bundle, obviously a heavy object, wrapped in cloth. He comes in,
sets the bundle down carefully on the table, and wipes his brow.)*

BIELDFELDT: I have something really remarkable to show
you, Herr Gynt. The workers found it today, in the

northwest quadrant. Something extraordinary. I have never seen anything quite like it. Truly astonishing.

PEER: What is it?

BIELDFELDT: A carving. It must have been done for a high royal personage. Perhaps even the Emperor himself. Perhaps even the last Emperor, Atahualpa.

PEER: Ah, Bieldfeldt, you rascal. Now you've really piqued my interest. An Emperor! Atahualpa! I may not be able to part with this. I may have to keep it for myself. Well, enough preamble. Unwrap the damn thing, and let's take a look.

BIELDFELDT: Wait. Just a moment, please.

PEER: Herr Doktor Bieldfeldt, if you're trying to drive up the price, such obvious sales techniques are really not necessary. If the object is as splendid as you say it is—

BIELDFELDT: No, no, that's not it at all. Before I show you what I have, I must warn you.

PEER: Warn me?

BIELDFELDT: Yes. Warn you.

PEER: What on earth about?

BIELDFELDT: The Quechua say the Incas put a curse on this piece. They say whoever looks upon this piece who is not of the highest royal Inca lineage is doomed to go mad. The power, the intensity, the sheer horror of what they see is too great to bear.

PEER: Don't be stupid, man. You're a scientist. Surely you don't give creedence to such superstitious nonsense?

BIELDFELDT: You scoff, but I'm quite serious, Herr Gynt. And I give you fair warning. I myself think there is something to what the Indians say. First, it was uncovered from an undisturbed tomb, a crypt which was in perfect condition, highly unusual—

PEER: What's so unusual about an undisturbed tomb?

BIELDFELDT: The site has been all around heavily plundered by grave robbers. But this one tomb alone was left untouched.

PEER: They missed it, that's all. Dumb luck.

BIELDFELDT: Perhaps. But I don't think so. I think the grave robbers deliberately shied away. And once the tomb was opened and the carving uncovered, the Indian diggers took one look and fled in horror.

PEER: Superstitious savages.

BIELDFELDT: Again, perhaps. But the man who found it, just this morning, has suffered a complete nervous collapse, and died no more than a few minutes ago, frothing at the mouth.

PEER: Sounds more like snakebite than an ancient Inca curse.

BIELDFELDT: There have been several other serious mishaps since this morning. Near-fatal accidents. The whole camp is in a panic. They demand it be taken away from the site immediately.

PEER: Folklore. Makes a good tale. It'll drive up the asking price. If I decide to sell it. Now will you show it to me? Or do I have to unveil it myself?

BIELDFELDT: Be my guest. But please allow me to leave the premises, first. I've already seen it, and the damn thing gives me chills.

PEER: Not so fast, Herr Doktor Bieldfeldt. I insist you remain a moment while I take a look.

(PEER *unwraps the object, with, despite his bravado, a certain amount of trepidation.*)

PEER: An ancient Inca curse. My goodness, that's a new one on me. Ah!

(*Revealed is a magnificent carved crystal skull.* PEER *holds it up to the light.* BIELDFELDT *cringes and looks away.*)

PEER: Fantastic! Crystal! See the way it breaks the light into a thousand rainbows! A skull! Perhaps modeled and carved on Atahualpa's own! Could it be? Yes? I think so. No question. I am looking into the eyes of Atahualpa himself! Amazing! I'll wager he had it carved specifically to confront the spectre of his own death! What do you think? Now, there's a gesture for you. A beau geste! Worthy of an emperor! Ah. Look deeply! Herein lie the secrets of the last of the Incas.

BIELDFELDT: Do you want it?

PEER: Of course I want it! Are you mad? Whatever you want for it, I'll pay!

BIELDFELDT: A thousand dollars—

PEER: A thousand dollars? Is that all? It's worth ten times that! Or more!

BIELDFELDT: A thousand dollars, if you agree to take it away by morning. Far away.

PEER: Done!

BIELDFELDT: My money now, if you please, Herr Gynt.

PEER: But we've never before insisted on such formalities—

BIELDFELDT: I must insist you pay me now.

PEER: Very well.

(He sets the skull down on the table, takes a bag of gold out of his desk and tosses it to BIELDFELDT.*)*

BIELDFELDT: Danke. Goodnight. God save you, Herr Gynt.

PEER: And you, Herr Doktor Bieldfeldt.

*(*BIELDFELDT *leaves as fast as he can.* PEER *takes a swig from the bottle of rum, goes back to the table, sits down, and picks up the skull, turning it in his hands.)*

PEER: Magnificent. I feel faint. Must be the air. So thin here in the high Andes. I see what Doctor Bieldfeldt meant. The thing's uncanny. The eyes. Look at the eyes. Not eyes, of course. Mockeries of eyes. Mere sockets. Still. Gives me chills, too.

(He hurriedly takes another swig.)

PEER: If I weren't a scientific, rational, modern American man, I could almost believe— *(Beat)* Even if there is a curse on this thing, it has nothing to do with me, Peer Gynt. It belongs to a vanished and vanquished world, a savage, superstitious empire that perished at the hands of its mirror image, the cruel Conquistadors, its pagan religion scattered to the four winds by the grace of true Christian faith—and force of superior arms.

(He holds it closer to the light.)

PEER: Carved by an anonymous artisan, a slave, no doubt. At the behest of an absolute despot. What must it have been like? To have been Emperor of the Incas, a being of absolute power, godlike, his people subject to his every whim and fancy. How I envy him! I see what these empty eyes have seen. I see it now. I see it all. Everything.

(The skull glows blood red.)

PEER: The whole history of Atahualpa's race is contained herein. All the wars and conquests. The gold. The blood. The slavery and human sacrifice. I see it. I see it. I see it clearly—

(He stares, transfixed. Blood begins to pour from the empty eye sockets. It flows over PEER's hands. PEER sees something before him and puts down the skull.)

PEER: Who's there?

VOICE: You have killed me, Peer!

PEER: The Old Man of the Forest! Sasquatch!

VOICE: You, Peer! You have shot me dead!

PEER: I? Not I! Not Peer!

VOICE: I bleed! See my wound! Touch me!

(In a daze, PEER rises from the table, reaches out his hand. To his amazement, a handful of rubies appear in his palm. He pours them onto the table. They flash in the light.)

PEER: Rubies!

VOICE: Here, Peer! This is what you wanted!

(The skull bleeds, the VOICES swirl around PEER, and he staggers and collapses, in a dead faint.)

Scene Six

(A small, white-washed cell in the Lima loony bin. PEER sits slumped against a wall on a crude wooden bench, trussed up in a straight jacket. From somewhere far above, a shaft of sunlight penetrates the gloom. A door opens, and a dapper older gentleman appears. DR ALVAREZ.)

DR ALVAREZ: *Buenas dias.* I am Dr Alvarez. How are you feeling today?

PEER: Where am I?

DR ALVAREZ: Lima. The Sanitorium of Our Lady of Sorrows.

PEER: Why?

DR ALVAREZ: You were brought here. By a— *(Consults his notes)* gentleman of German nationality. Doctor Bieldfeldt? An archeologist, working in Machu Picchu?

PEER: Ah, yes. I recall the fellow. How long have I been here?

DR ALVAREZ: A week. You've been delirious. Out of your mind with fever.

PEER: What happened?

DR ALVAREZ: Apparently you suffered a nervous collapse.

PEER: Just my malaria, kicking up.

DR ALVAREZ: Ah, well, we shall see. It is possible.

PEER: No, I'm convinced. I had fever, I was hallucinating. Is this straitjacket necessary?

DR ALVAREZ: Oh, I'm sorry. I beg your pardon. Allow me.

(He goes to PEER, loosens his restraints.)

DR ALVAREZ: Your convulsions were such, when you were admitted, we were afraid you would harm yourself. You swallowed your tongue. We retrieved it for you. It wasn't easy. I can tell you that. The tongue is a slippery thing—

PEER: Thank you very much, I'm sure.

DR ALVAREZ: Not at all. It was our duty. All in a day's work. There.

(He pulls the straitjacket off. PEER stretches, gratefully.)

PEER: Ah! That's better! Thank you, doctor.

DR ALVAREZ: How are you feeling now?

PEER: Weak. Stiff. Sore. But otherwise okay. Hunky-dory. Peachy keen. When can I go?

DR ALVAREZ: We'll keep you here a few days, make sure the malaria, if that's what it was, has subsided.

PEER: Malaria. What else could it be? So there's no need to— *(Remembers)* Doctor!

DR ALVAREZ: What? What is it, Senor Gynt?

PEER: Where are my things? My bags? Where are they?

DR ALVAREZ: We have them here. They are safe.

PEER: Can you arrange for them to be brought to me?

DR ALVAREZ: Certainly—

PEER: This minute, I mean. It's most important. I would be eternally in your debt.

DR ALVAREZ: As you wish.

(DR ALVAREZ *goes out.* PEER *paces, nervously.*)

PEER: If anything's happened to that skull, heads will roll. A small joke. My own little empire's probably falling to pieces in my absence. Sloth. Incompetence. Embezzlement. It never fails. If you want something done right, you have to do it yourself. Oh, to be Emperor of all the Incas. With the power of life and death! Instead of firing an incompetent employee—summary execution! The idea is an attractive one.

(DR ALVAREZ *returns, followed by an* ORDERLY, *who carts in* PEER's *things.*)

PEER: Ah! Thank God! Let's see here!

(*He roots through his things. Finds the bundle wrapped in rags. Hefts it.*)

PEER: Here it is. Feels intact. Doctor Alvarez.

DR ALVAREZ: *Si*, Señor Gynt.

PEER: You seem a trustworthy fellow.

DR ALVAREZ: Señor Gynt, if I give you my word, it is a matter of honor.

PEER: You certainly come from a different world than I do, Doctor. We always have our fingers crossed. Will you do something for me?

DR ALVAREZ: If it is within my power.

PEER: I would like you to box this object and ship it to Dr Bridewell, at the British Museum in London. Tell him it's from me, and to remit the purchase price to my bank account here in Lima. Tell him ten thousand pounds, and not a penny less! Can you do that for me?

DR ALVAREZ: Certainly. That is not a problem. But ten thousand pounds—that is a small fortune, Señor.

PEER: Would you like to see what it is?

DR ALVAREZ: Of course, I am curious.

PEER: Then take a look.

(PEER *unwraps the bundle, hands the skull to* DR ALVAREZ, *who gasps.*)

DR ALVAREZ: Magnificent! Inca?

PEER: What else? Worth every penny, don't you think?

DR ALVAREZ: Without a doubt. I'm no expert, but I would say so, yes. Exquisite! Who is it? Do you know?

PEER: Atahualpa.

DR ALVAREZ: Really! The last Emperor. Oh, my.

PEER: It must have been my malaria! It must have been!

DR ALVAREZ: What is that, Señor?

PEER: I saw the entire history of the Incas through those horrible empty eyes. The rise and fall of their Empire. The conquests. The coming of Pizarro. I saw how civilization, all civilization everywhere, is built upon a pyramid of human blood.

(DR ALVAREZ *stares into the eye sockets of the skull.*)

DR ALVAREZ: You saw all that?

PEER: I did. I thought I did.

DR ALVAREZ: And that is what caused your collapse?

PEER: My malaria caused my collapse. The fever. Tell me, Doctor, are you affected by what you see when you look into those eyes?

DR ALVAREZ: I see nothing at all, my friend. But then, I'm not a trained observer. I'm not even really a doctor.

PEER: You're not?

DR ALVAREZ: Oh, no. I'm a patient. Like yourself. There's been a revolution, you see. And the inmates and jailers have switched places. A pleasant turnabout, if you ask me. I get to wear this white coat, and people treat me seriously. Call me doctor. Very nice.

PEER: Then I'm free to go.

DR ALVAREZ: If you wish. But I would not advise it. The streets are not safe for foreigners.

ORDERLY: Corpses clog the gutters. The streets and storm sewers run red with blood.

DR ALVAREZ: It's true. I'm afraid they do. You had better stay with us until things settle down and life returns to normal.

PEER: I'm your prisoner.

DR ALVAREZ: Our honored guest. In the meantime, I will send this to the British Museum. Señor Gynt? Can you tell me how? I am a long time away from the workings of the day-to-day world—

PEER: Try the Embassy. Diplomatic pouch.

DR ALVAREZ: Ah! Good idea. Pouch the skull.
How delightful *Buenas dias*, Señor.

PEER: *Gracias*, Doctor.

DR ALVAREZ: *De nada.*

(DR ALVAREZ *and the* ORDERLY *take the skull and leave.*)

PEER: He'll probably steal it. Too bad. I could use the money. The British Museum would pay a pretty penny. If he's smart, he'll sell it to them himself and cut me out completely. Ah, well. You can't trust anyone in this world.

(*He finds the velvet bag, pulls the shrunken heads out of it, arranges them in a row.*)

PEER: Gentlemen. How nice to see you. I'm in a good mood this evening. In spite of my circumstances. I'm in a pickle, it's true. But nothing like the predicament you put me in. Still, I've always had the last laugh, haven't I? Always. Here I am—Emperor of these four walls! Emperor of myself, when all is said and done! Lovely! I'm in such a forgiving mood, this evening! Allow me to serenade you. What would you like to hear? Something of the country perhaps? Certainly. I hope you like it. In fact, I wrote it myself.

(*He finds his guitar, picks it up and starts to play, a sweet song. He sings softly in gibberish Spanish. His eyes gleam with a quiet madness. Clearly, he's far from cured. Something rattles in the guitar. He stops playing, turns it over and shakes it. Rubies fall out of the guitar. He picks one up, holds it up to the light, horrified. Behind him, in the shaft of sunlight,* SALLY *appears,*) *gazing into the middle distance, watching the horizon, waiting for* PEER. *As* PEER *picks up the rubies one by one, stunned, the lights fade to black.)*

END ACT FOUR

ACT FIVE

Scene One

(*On the deck of a ship sailing off the coast of Washington State. It is sunset, and the wind is stiff and the weather threatening. PEER is now an old man, but strong as an ox, with snow-white hair and beard. He wears seafarer's clothing, and he looks weather-beaten and hardened. He stands next to the* CAPTAIN, *at the wheel, and the* FIRST MATE. PEER *looks towards land and picks out the peaks of the Olympics.*)

PEER: There's Mount Olympus. There's Quinalt, and Queets, and Mount Seattle, and Old Tom. Shining in the storm light. Nothing lasts forever, eh? Only the earth and the mountains.

CAPTAIN: True enough.

PEER: Wind's picked up.

CAPTAIN: It's gonna blow tonight. We're in for stormy weather, sure.

PEER: Can we see Mount Tahoma from here?

CAPTAIN: No, it's hid behind the Olympics there. So, you're familiar with these parts, I see.

PEER: I grew up here.

CAPTAIN: Whereabouts?

PEER: Near the Puget Sound. Will we make the Strait of Juan de Fuca by daybreak?

CAPTAIN: Let's hope. If the weather doesn't get too goddamn bad, we should.

PEER: Remind me, Captain, when we come to settle up. I'd like to give a little something to the crew.

CAPTAIN: That's kind of you, sir.

PEER: Won't be much. Ain't got much. You wouldn't know it to look at me, but I had money once. Lots of it. A fortune. I was a millionaire seven times over. Seven times seven times over. But I lost it. Bad luck and trouble—

CAPTAIN: Well, that won't matter, if you're going home—

PEER: My people are gone. No one to greet me at the dock. No embarrassing displays of emotion. I'm an old dog, a mangy stray.

CAPTAIN: Storm's picking up. Gonna be a rip-snorter.

PEER: Are you worried?

CAPTAIN: Nothing we can't handle. I've been through far worse.

PEER: You've got a first-rate crew, Captain. I'll be glad to give them something extra for their pains.

CAPTAIN: They'll be obliged to you, sir. Most of 'em have a hard time making ends meet. It's tough to keep a wife and kids in shoes and socks on what a sailor makes.

PEER: What? They're married? It never crossed my mind—

CAPTAIN: Like I said, most of 'em. Think of all those families watching the sky and waiting anxiously for the men to make it home.

PEER: The hell with them.

CAPTAIN: What's that, you say?

PEER: They got wives waiting for them, dinner on the table, and packs of runny-nosed brats running to hug them when they come through the front door, the hell with them! They'll not get an extra penny out of me! I've got nobody and no one, and that's a fact.

CAPTAIN: Suit yourself, sir. It was your idea. Now, if you'll excuse me, I've got a boat to run and a storm to weather.

(The CAPTAIN leaves. The FIRST MATE takes the wheel. PEER stares glumly out to sea.)

PEER: A wife and kids. Happy to see you when you come home from a long journey. When have I ever had that? In all my travels, I've never had anyone's good wishes. No one's missed me, no one's ever given a second thought to poor Peer. Where is he? How's he faring? When's he coming back? No one. Never. They could all care less.

I know what I'll do! I'll throw a party for the crew! Get
them all snockered! That'll spoil their happy homecoming!
Get 'em all oiled up and stinking drunk! They'll stagger
home in the middle of the night, reeking of booze and
vomit, dinner gone cold on the table hours ago. That'll
fix 'em! Instead of happy families, there'll be tears and
recriminations. Beatings and broken crockery. I'll spike
their wheels!

(The ship lurches suddenly, and PEER *stumbles.)*

PEER: What a sea!

CAPTAIN: *(Off)* Ahoy! A wreck to leeward! Three men on a
raft! Lower a boat! Hurry!

FIRST MATE: In these swells? It'll swamp faster than you can
say William Jennings Bryan!

PEER: If you're men, you'll try to save them.

FIRST MATE: Can't be done in seas like this. Why should we
risk our lives for nothing? Those poor bastards haven't got
a chance. Look!

(They look.)

FIRST MATE: They've gone under already, poor bastards,
what'd I tell you? Before we could do anything foolish on
their behalf. Gone to the widow maker. Three more brand
new widows and who knows how many orphans in the
world. Happens fast.

(PEER moves away.)

PEER: What a night. You can't trust your brother, it's every
man for himself, and God can't hear you over the howling
wind. When I get back home, I'll retrieve the farm by hook
or crook. Once they find out who I am, once I reveal my
true identity, they'll greet me like the prodigal son, make
a fuss, flatter me 'til the cows come home. Let them try to
butter me up. I'll be damned if I let anyone come across my
threshhold and warm themselves by my fire, or stuff their
faces from my larder. Let them beg on bended knee, they
won't get so much as a plugged nickel from me.

(The MYSTERIOUS STRANGER *appears out of the fog and stands
next to* PEER.)

MYSTERIOUS STRANGER: Good evening.

PEER: Evening. Who are you? I don't recall seeing you before. I came aboard at San Francisco—

MYSTERIOUS STRANGER: I was already aboard.

PEER: Oh. Really. I thought I was the only passenger. My mistake.

MYSTERIOUS STRANGER: Don't worry about it. You could not have known. I never leave my cabin by day.

PEER: You don't mind my saying so, you don't look so well. You're gray as a ghost. Seasick?

MYSTERIOUS STRANGER: On the contrary. I'm healthy as an ox. I'll live forever. I love this weather, don't you? Quite a storm.

PEER: It's getting pretty rough. It's always rough up here. Cape Desolation. Aptly named.

MYSTERIOUS STRANGER: Thank goodness.

PEER: Thank goodness? Why do you say that?

MYSTERIOUS STRANGER: Look at those swells. Waves as tall as full-grown Douglas firs. Think of all the wrecks we'll have tonight! All the corpses washing ashore! All the new-made widows and orphans! How delicious!

PEER: Heaven forbid. Are you crazy?

MYSTERIOUS STRANGER: Have you ever seen a man drown? Or hanged? Or strangled?

PEER: Can't say as I have, thank God.

MYSTERIOUS STRANGER: It's an interesting thing. Corpses grin. Oh, yes, they do. They clench their teeth, they bite their tongues straight through. It's the rictus!

PEER: I didn't know that.

MYSTERIOUS STRANGER: The rictus! That's what does it! What's your opinion, sir? Think we'll founder on the rocks?

PEER: I certainly hope not.

MYSTERIOUS STRANGER: This channel's tricky. We'll never see the lighthouse beam through the fog. It's a Devil's brew tonight.

PEER: Devil's brew. Ugh. Don't say that.

MYSTERIOUS STRANGER: Look here, my friend. Suppose you drown, and I don't.

PEER: What a thought! What are you talking about?

MYSTERIOUS STRANGER: Let me have your corpse, will you?

PEER: My corpse? Are you mad?

MYSTERIOUS STRANGER: If you'd be so kind. In the interests of science, you understand. I'd be ever so grateful to you.

PEER: Go away! Get away from me!

MYSTERIOUS STRANGER: They'll open you up, and let the daylight in. You see, sir, I'm trying to find where dreams begin, their abode, where they lurk and breed, so to speak. And you look like a dreamer to me. A definite dreamer, yes, indeed!

PEER: Leave me alone!

MYSTERIOUS STRANGER: But my dear sir, you have no idea how valuable a drowned man and his water-logged corpse are to a fellow like me—

PEER: I know what you are. You're a damned Jonah! You'll cause the ship to run aground with your blasphemous chatter!

MYSTERIOUS STRANGER: I can see you're not in the mood to discuss this rationally. We'll meet again when you're drowning. You'll come around to my way of thinking, mark my words.

(The MYSTERIOUS STRANGER bows and goes.)

PEER: Scientists have become more and more sinister, don't you think?

(He moves back to the FIRST MATE.)

PEER: Did you see that passenger?

FIRST MATE: Sir?

PEER: What's his name? Do you know?

FIRST MATE: You're the only passenger aboard, so far as I know.

PEER: Damn. This gets more alarming by the moment.

FIRST MATE: (Shouting) We're coming up on the reef!
All hands on deck!

(Shouts and cries of confusion and alarm, over the storm.)

PEER: My things! My trunk! My strong box! My money! Get them up above from down below! Get them to the lifeboats!

FIRST MATE: Sorry, sir. You'll have to fend for yourself.
We need all hands on deck—

(*The* CAPTAIN *rushes on.*)

CAPTAIN: We're going aground! Man the lifeboats!
Hold her steady 'til we hit! Courage, man!

FIRST MATE: Aye aye, sir—

(*The ship hits with a great shudder and a terrible noise.*)

CAPTAIN: She's breaking up! Abandon ship!

(*Noise and confusion. Everyone scrambles to get away.*)

Scene Two

(PEER *is clinging to an overturned lifeboat, off the coast.*)

PEER: Help! Help! Help, I'm drowning! Save me, God!
Can you hear me? Not listening, as usual! Deaf as a post!
As usual! Help!

(*The* COOK *appears, grabs on to the boat and threatens to sink it.*)

COOK: Help me!

PEER: Let go! What do you think you're doing? You'll
drown us both!

COOK: Let go yourself!

PEER: She'll only take one! Let go! Let go, damn you!

(*They fight.*)

COOK: I've got a wife and family! There's no one to mourn
for you, you old fart—

PEER: So what? What difference does that make?

COOK: My children need me! Let go!

PEER: I need to live more than you do—I don't have any
children yet—you've done your part for propagation,
you're through—have the good manners to let go
gracefully—

COOK: You let go! I'm young! I'm only a poor cook!
You're old, you used to be rich, you've had your life—

PEER: It's not over yet! And I mean to be rich again! Let go!
Don't be afraid! Drowning's quick, you won't suffer—

COOK: Have mercy, I beg you—
(The COOK *slips off.)*
COOK: Help! I'm drowning! Help!
PEER: Wait! Grab my hand!
(The COOK *grabs* PEER's *hand.)*
PEER: Now say your prayers.
COOK: Our Father, who art in Heaven—
PEER: Very good—
COOK: I can't remember the rest, it's all gone dark—
PEER: Doesn't matter, we get your drift—
COOK: Give us this day our daily bread—
PEER: Ah, a cook to the end. Amen.
(He lets go the COOK's *hand, and the* COOK *slips under and drowns.)*
PEER: True to himself to the last. Good lad.
(The MYSTERIOUS STRANGER *floats alongside the boat.)*
MYSTERIOUS STRANGER: Hello. Ah. Taking on water, I see.
PEER: Oh, my God. It's you.
MYSTERIOUS STRANGER: Told you we'd meet again. Now. About your corpse.
PEER: Get away from me. Who are you?
MYSTERIOUS STRANGER: Just a friendly fellow passenger.
PEER: A likely story. You're no friendly passenger. You stink of sulphur and brimstone. And how can you swim with that hoof you've got for a foot? Doesn't it drag you under?
MYSTERIOUS STRANGER: Oh, please. Don't be melodramatic. I'm merely a messenger of light.
PEER: A messenger of light? Oh, that's a good one. I'd laugh, if I weren't afraid of drowning.
MYSTERIOUS STRANGER: You shouldn't be afraid of drowning. Just let go. Follow the beautiful light at the end of the corridor. It's easy. You'll feel ever so much better. It's so restful.
PEER: Are you trying to get me to loose my grip? Well, I won't listen to you, my friend. Now, get away from me.

I'm going to live. I'm going to make it to shore. And you
are not going to stop me. Do you hear?
MYSTERIOUS STRANGER: Oh, well. Don't get excited.
You totally misunderstand my intent. As far as that goes,
everyone knows the eponymous character never dies in
the middle of the last act. *(He disappears.)*
PEER: Wonder what he meant by that?
(The lights fade out on PEER, *clinging to his life raft.)*

Scene Three

*(A funeral at the graveyard outside town. The townsfolk,
including* PREACHER ROWE, SMITTY *and his* PALS, JOHN
JOHNSON, BAKER, *etc. are there, now grown very old.* PEER
watches from the edge of the crowd. PREACHER ROWE *is still
potted, after all these years.)*
PREACHER ROWE: We now commend this good woman to
your safekeeping, Lord. May God have mercy on her soul.
Amen.
ALL: Amen.
PREACHER ROWE: Let's have a drink.
ALL: Amen.
(The crowd begins to break up. PEER *tugs on* BAKER'S *sleeve.)*
PEER: Whose funeral?
BAKER: Ingrid. Wife of Smitty.
PEER: Smitty?
BAKER: Right over there. The grieving widower.
PEER: Oh, yes. So Ingrid married Smitty, after all.
Fancy that.
BAKER: You know Ingrid and Smitty?
PEER: Oh, no, no. I just—
*(*SMITTY, *dressed in mourning black, sees* PEER *and comes over.)*
SMITTY: So, we have a stranger here.
PEER: Yes. Just passing through. Thought I'd pay my
respects. Hope you don't mind.
SMITTY: Welcome. Though it's a sad occasion.

PEER: You know what they say. No one gets out of here alive.

SMITTY: That's true, friend. That's true. When your time's up, it's up. The bell tolls for everyone in the end.

PEER: My condolences. I didn't know your wife—

SMITTY: She was a good woman. She was disgraced when I married her, but she turned out alright. Quit her wild ways, settled down.

PEER: Disgraced? I don't mean to pry—

SMITTY: Oh, no. It's common knowledge, round about. When she was young, she run off with a fella named Peer Gynt and left her intended, not me, but John Johnson yonder, cooling his heels at the altar.

JOHN JOHNSON: I wouldn't take her back, not me. Not after what she done on what was 'sposed to be our wedding night. Not in her condition.

SMITTY: Your loss, my gain, John, I always said.

PEER: What condition was that, if you don't mind me asking?

SMITTY: Knocked up, in a word. Six months after we were married, she bore a bouncing baby boy.

PEER: A boy!

SMITTY: Named Peter.

PEER: Another one! Fancy that!

SMITTY: Another one, what do you mean?

PEER: Oh, nothing, nothing. Kind of you to be a father to the kid.

SMITTY: He's a good boy. I love him like my own. Takes after his mother, thank the Lord. Honest as the day is long. Not like the bastard who begat him.

PEER: Peer Gynt?

SMITTY: That's the one. None other.

PEER: And what was he? Besides a bastard?

SMITTY: A world-class liar, mostly.

PEER: How so?

ALL: How so? Hear that? He wants to know how Peer Gynt was a liar!

BAKER: Peer Gynt was to liars what Paul Bunyan was to lumberjacks! What Babe the Blue Ox was to your run-of-the-mill Bessie milk cow! What Pecos Bill was to saddle-tramps and cowpokes!

FIRST PAL: He claimed he could fly. He claimed he could turn himself invisible.

SECOND PAL: He claimed he could bottle up the Devil himself and make Old Scratch jump through hoops of his devising.

THIRD PAL: He'd claim just about anything and do it with a straight face and all the God given conviction in the world!

BAKER: You never seen such a liar in all your born days.

PEER: And what happened to this remarkable fellow?

JOHN JOHNSON: He went abroad. Hoping to strike it rich.

PEER: And did he?

JOHN JOHNSON: Nope. Came to a bad end. Hanged himself in some loony bin down South America ways.

BAKER: I heard he died in a drunk tank in Panama. Croaked without a penny to his name.

PEER: A fitting end for a world-class liar, either way.

(PETER GYNT *enters, a grown man of forty-five. He throws his arms around* SMITTY.)

PETER: Come on, Pa. Funeral's over. Let's go down to the White Eagle and have the wake. Crack open the whiskey, remember my Ma, and auction off what's left of Peer Gynt to the four winds.

SMITTY: You're welcome to join us, stranger.

PEER: Perhaps I'll follow along later. What's all this about an auction?

SMITTY: Peter's Ma left him a trunk, full of odds and ends she got from his Grandma Hannah. All that's left of the old bastard.

PEER: Like what, for instance?

PETER: Oh, all kinds of marvels. His cloak of invisibility—

BAKER: It's invisible alright. The moths have been chewing on it so damn long there's nothing left but buttons and collar.

PETER: Then there's the antlers of the famous flying buck—

JOHN JOHNSON: Doe, is more like it. I seen bigger points on a jackalope.

PETER: And there's the bottle Peer trapped the Devil in, which my daddy was persuaded to open, against his better judgment—

PEER: Is that true?

SMITTY: Mister, if you believe that, you believe in Haints. Nothin' more'n a common patent medicine bottle, I assure you. With a cork that don't fit.

PETER: And last, but not least, a mold he used for casting silver buttons—

SMITTY: Now there's something practical. At last!

PETER: Although he used to claim, naturally enough, that his buttons were worth a fortune, and of course they weren't worth much more than one thin dime—

PEER: I should hold an auction of all my leftovers.

SMITTY: Yeah? Like what?

PEER: Oh, my entire empire, for starters. Palaces and diamond mines and canefields and all the daydreams you could imagine. And a crown of fool's gold, for anyone who cares to put it on. Not to mention my collection of genuine shrunken heads. Former business associates who came, like your lying friend, to a bad end.

(The others stare at him for a moment. Then:)

SMITTY: Well, old man, you're welcome at the wake, if you've a mind to come.

(PEER nods. The others drift out, leaving PEER alone.)

Scene Four

(Twilight. A clearing in the woods. PEER is rooting in the dirt for wild onions.)

PEER: So it's come to this. Rooting in the earth for wild onions like a feral pig. How far I've come. No more cognac for me. I never did learn to catch salmon like the grizzlies, more's the pity. You can't fill your belly on beans and wild onions, when all is said and done. Ah! Here's one. *(He plucks an onion out of the dirt, sits, and starts to peel it.)* When I die, which won't be long now, at this rate, they can bury me under yonder tree and carve in its bark: "Here lies Peer Gynt, Emperor of the Groundhogs". *(He laughs.)* Peer, you're nothing but fortune's fool. Just a poor wild onion, nothing more. And now, Peer, I'm going to peel you, layer by layer, and see what's really there. *(He peels the onion, one layer at a time.)* The battered outer skin, that's a whole life of hard knocks and misfortune. This next one's the old man who knows not a living soul in the whole world. This one's the shipwreck, a little waterlogged. This one's the fur trapper in the Yukon, with a bit of pure Peer juice left. This one's the peddler, going from town to town selling snake oil across America. This one's the poor lunatic, imprisoned in Lima, Peru. This one's the Emperor of the Amazon, fresh and tangy, stinking of lies. So many layers, where's the center? Here's the shiftless youth, the ne'er do well, the braggart, the daydreamer. Look at this, they just get smaller and smaller, until— *(He's come to the center of the onion, and there's nothing left.)* Oh, my God. Look at that. Nothing left but scraps. Nothing there at the center at all. Ain't nature grand! Enough to give a body chills. *(He throws the scraps of the onion aside.)* The hell with this morbid way of thinking! Life's tough, that's all, so what? You play the hand that's dealt you! And if it all adds up to the scrapheap in the end—

(He hears singing. A woman's voice. He goes to the edge of the clearing and looks down the hill.)

PEER: I know that voice. And I know that house. Built up in yonder willow tree. I've seen it before. I've been here before. But where am I?

(SALLY appears in a shaft of light, singing a folk song about a woman waiting for her true love to come back to her. PEER recoils in recognition.)

PEER: Sally. She remembered her promise. And I forgot
mine. I put it clear out of my mind. She promised to wait,
and I promised to come back. She stayed true to her word,
and I didn't. I'm an emperor, alright. The Emperor of Sorry.
(He runs out. SALLY disappears.)

Scene Five

*(A clear-cut and a massive burn. Nothing but blackened stumps
and spars. Patches of low-lying white fog. PEER comes wandering
in.)*

PEER: Well, here's a landscape matches my mood. They've
clear-cut this whole mountainside and left the rest to burn.
Lightning, most like. Look at this devastation! Charcoal
and ashes, for miles, and not a living soul. Perfect. This is
what my dreams and schemes and lies have come to. I'll
build a house of cards here on the shifting ash, and inscribe
my motto over the door: "Lie like hell, and never say
you're sorry." I'll be king of the hill!

(He laughs bitterly, then stops, listening.)

PEER: What's that sound? Like kids, crying. What's this?
Tumbleweeds! Tumbleweeds! It's the tumbleweeds making
that awful, mournful sound. Get outa here! Go away!
Leave me be! Everybody knows tumbleweeds are really
witches! Haints! Shape-shifters! Go on! Leave me be!

TUMBLEWEEDS: Peer! We are the thoughts you should have
thought! The things you should have done! We are the
hopes you should have had! We are the songs you should
have sung!

PEER: Nonsense! I done plenty in my life! More 'n most
men! Don't condemn me for what I *haven't* done. Leave
me be! Leave me to my kingdom of ash!

*(The TUMBLEWEEDS roll away. MR BONES, an elegant
gentleman in evening dress appears.)*

MR BONES: Good evening. How nice to see you.

PEER: And you, sir.

MR BONES: Are you on your way somewhere?

PEER: To a funeral, is all.

MR BONES: My eyesight isn't what it used to be. Pardon me, but isn't your name Peer?

PEER: Peer Gynt, that's right.

MR BONES: What do you know? Just the fellow I'm looking for this evening. Peer Gynt. How about that?

PEER: Why? What do you want me for?

MR BONES: Oh, I'm here to fetch you. It's time.

PEER: Time for what?

MR BONES: It's your time, Peer. Time's up. Time to go. Hear the bell tolling? You're to be reunited.

PEER: Reunited?

MR BONES: Mmmm. How to put this. Reunited. With the Eternal Voice. The Oceanic Feeling. The Great Universal. You're to be dissolved. Returned to whence you came. Put back in the stew, and we'll try again. Rather like those silver buttons you made as a child. To put it plainly, you're to be melted down.

PEER: Oh, no. I've always been a loner. I don't think I care to be mixed up and melted down and added in with everyone else.

MR BONES: Oh, not everyone goes back in the pot. The best and the worst are saved for other uses.

PEER: Isn't this kind of short notice? I don't think it's fair.

MR BONES: Not at all. We've been preparing for this day for a long time. Everything's ready for you. The coffin's built, the grave's dug, the worms have on their bibs. It's time.

PEER: But nobody told me.

MR BONES: Well, that's the way it is with life and death, isn't it? The day's chosen in secret, and nobody bothers to clue in the guest of honor. That way it's always a surprise. Now, hurry up. I have orders from on high to fetch your soul right now and don't dawdle.

PEER: I'm dizzy. Who did you say you were?

MR BONES: Mister Bones, they call me.

PEER: So this is it, eh, Peer? The Day of Reckoning. You know, I'm not such a bad guy, when you look at what

I've actually done. I've got my share of good deeds on the books. I mean, the most anyone can say against me is I've told a few whoppers, stretched the truth on occasion, been a little bit lazy in my day and given to idle speculation, but I'm not what you can call a real criminal. I'm not a bonafide big-time sinner, not by a long shot.

MR BONES: You've hit the button on the nose, my friend. So to speak. You're not really any kind of sinner at all, not in our book. Which is why you get to skip all the hellfire and brimstone, and go right back in the stew. Lucky you.

PEER: Stew or brimstone, I know you now! Away from me, Devil! Lucifer! Satan! I renounce you.

MR BONES: Oh, dear, Peer. Do I look like I have hooves? Should I remove my shoes and show you?

PEER: If you're who I take you for, it's no great trick for you to make your hoof look like any normal foot, so just be on your cloven way.

MR BONES: My friend, you're making a big mistake in not coming quietly. I've told you the lay of the land. You're not much of a sinner—

PEER: That's true enough—

MR BONES: But I wouldn't call you a saint, either.

PEER: Nor would I—

MR BONES: Not even particularly good, or virtuous, or upstanding. In fact, you've played both sides against the middle your whole life and ended up betwixt and between, neither truly bad nor truly good, but just getting by, cutting corners and watering the whiskey. Now I've told you how it has to be. We spare you the barbecue and brimstone, but back in the pot you go. The Maker hates to waste raw materials. You didn't turn out the way He'd hoped, you had a screw or two loose and a piece or two missing, like a silver button without the loop at the back to make it truly functional. You were shiny alright, but you didn't amount to much in the end. So we'll melt you down, and try again.

PEER: Since I'm so worthless, why not just let me go?

MR BONES: I told you, the Maker needs your soul, grubby as it is, it's worth something, it's got Divine Spark, we can't just throw that away—

PEER: No, no, no, you're not gonna toss me in with a bunch of John Does, and mix me up with them! I'll go kicking and screaming! Anything but that! I'd rather roast in Hell for all eternity than lose my Gyntish nature, be erased from the Book of Life, just like I'd never been born, what an insult!

MR BONES: My dear fellow, I believe you're laboring under a delusion. Your whole life you've never been yourself. Why start now? Why worry about it in death? It doesn't matter if you're erased, as you put it, since you've never even been.

PEER: You're the one's deluded, my friend. You mean to tell me Peer Gynt's been somebody else all this time? I don't believe I'll go along with that. Why if you could look inside me, you'd see Peer Gynt and not a trace of nothing else.

MR BONES: I have my orders right here—"Peer Gynt, round him up right now, and dump him in the soup before sundown."

PEER: Uh-huh, sir, wouldn't it be a crying shame if tomorrow they found out it was somebody else you were supposed to be putting in that Universal Stew of yours? A case of mistaken identity? No, sir, I just can't go along with you, I'm sorry. You're wasting your breath, pal.

MR BONES: Quit stalling, and come along.

PEER: Look, what if I proved to you that I'd been Peer Gynt my entire life, would that let me off the hook here?

MR BONES: Prove it how?

PEER: Witnesses.

MR BONES: I don't think the Maker would accept hearsay as evidence—

PEER: Well, we'll cross that bridge when we come to it. Look, just lend me to myself and give me time to prove to you that I shouldn't be melted down like so much scrap metal. Just a little more time to make my case, that's all I ask.

MR BONES: Alright. I'll meet you at the next crossroads. Better hurry. You haven't got much time.

(PEER *runs out.*)

Scene Six

(Deeper into the clear-cut. PEER *runs on.)*

PEER: Tick tock tick tock tick. The clock is ticking. I feel
it in my gut. Time is money, true enough. I need a witness.
I wonder if Mr Bones' crossroads are near or far. Near,
most likely. A witness, a witness, where shall I ever find a
witness? I'm in the middle of a howling wilderness here!
What a world! It's not easy to prove you are who you are.
Think about it!

(The KING *of the Mountains, now a wizened old man, shuffles in,
wearing a knapsack and using a cane.)*

KING: A penny, please, sir, for a poor old man.

PEER: Sorry. Ain't got a nickel to my name.

KING: Well, well, well. Look who's here! Peer Gynt!
Prince Peer, his own self. So, we meet again! Amazing!

PEER: I'm sorry, I don't recognize you.

KING: You don't recognize your almost father-in-law?
The King of the whole damn Big Rock Candy Mountain?

PEER: Well, I'll be damned! It is you, Your Highness! What
are you doing round these parts? And how did you come
to be in such sorry straits?

KING: I've fallen on hard times, my son. Evil days. I've lost
everything. My own children have robbed me blind and
cast me out in the cold, cruel world. I'm a drifter, plain and
simple, down on my luck.

PEER: No, this is lucky. A perfect witness. Someone who
knew me when.

KING: Speaking of which, I see you've gone gray.

PEER: Time spares no one, Dad. And while we're at it, let's
let sleeping dogs lie and speak not of days gone by. I was a
reckless youth—

KING: Ah, don't fret about that. You made the right choice,
spurning my girl. She went bad, took up with some two-bit
Haint from Sacramento. Now my grandson, on the other
hand, a chip off the old block, you'd be proud of him,

sowing his wild oats up and down the coast, must have
two dozen brats with his stumpy teeth and handsome
overhanging brow—

PEER: Pop, I hate to interrupt, especially since we ain't seen
each other since God knows when, but I have a favor to ask
of you. I need a statement from you, sorta like an affidavit.
If you'd oblige me, maybe I can see my way clear to loan
you a few bucks for booze—

KING: Oh, so I can do His Highness a favor, can I?

PEER: I'd be much obliged, in fact.

KING: Well, so long as I can get the same good word in turn
from you, I'll swear to anything.

PEER: It's a deal. All you have to do is swear that when
push came to shove, I turned down the opportunity to
become a Haint like you. I stood on my own two feet and
stayed true to myself. My Gyntish nature. And I gave up a
lot when I did that. A kingdom, a fortune, a family. Will
you swear that's what happened way back when?

KING: Nope.

PEER: Why not? Why the hell not?

KING: Cause that ain't what happened. You don't want me
to perjure myself, do you?

PEER: But that's the truth.

KING: You drank with us, you ate with us, you wore our
clothes, you got halfway down the aisle.

PEER: I was tempted, I allow. You were a wonderful host.
But I bailed out at the end. I just couldn't go through with it.

KING: But you did. You may have left my baby standing
at the altar, but you lit out of there with the Haint motto
engraved on your heart, and you've lived up to the spirit
and the letter of that precious sacred saying every day of
your life.

PEER: What motto's that? I don't remember.

KING: Do what you gotta do to get through.

PEER: So that's where I've heard that phrase before! Now
I remember. Do what you have to do to get through. Oh,
my God.

KING: Ungrateful boy. How sharper than a serpent's tooth. You've lived as a secret Haint instead of a truly human person all your life. You owe it all to me, and the motto we give you.

PEER: I'm sorry, I ain't no Haint! No matter what you say.

KING: Isn't it obvious? You've lived your life like one. You shoulda stayed with us, in the first place. Saved yourself all that traipsing around the world. Searching for God knows what. You already found your place with us.

PEER: You mean I should have settled down with the Haints on Big Rock Candy Mountain? Married your daughter? Peer Gynt a one-eyed Haint? Ridiculous! Here's a nickel for your troubles. Go away.

KING: Where'm I 'sposed to go?

PEER: I don't give a good goddamn. Go home.

KING: Ain't got no home. My grandkids say I don't exist. Call me legendary.

PEER: I know the feeling.

KING: Kith and kin are the worst, let's face it. Sure you can't loan me something more to get me on down the road?

PEER: Sorry. I'm flat out busted.

KING: Broke?

PEER: That too.

KING: My, my. His Highness is broke.

PEER: That's right. His Highness is broke. Comes of associating with the likes of you. You must have cursed me early on, cursed me my whole life.

KING: Wasn't us. Was your own nature done you in. Well, well, well. I was hoping to get something more outa you, my boy. Why I came looking for you. You have severely dashed my hopes in that direction. Guess there's nothing for me now but to head on down to San Francisco.

PEER: And when you get there?

KING: Go on the stage. Become a character actor. Maybe play King Lear on the great stage of the Geary Theater.

PEER: Good fortune to you. When you get there, give them my regards. Tell 'em I'm on my way. Maybe I'll write me a play. The story of my life. A comic farce. I'll call it *Peer Gynt—The True Story.*

(PEER *runs off, leaving the* KING *alone.*)

Scene Seven

(*A crossroads.* PEER *appears.*)

PEER: I'm in trouble now. That old man's "Do what you gotta do to get through" has signed, sealed and delivered me to the stew pot. What the hell! When the chips are down, and your boat's run aground, grab any old piece of wreckage and hang on for dear life!

(MR BONES *appears.*)

MR BONES: Well, Peer. Are your witnesses here?

PEER: A crossroads? So soon?

MR BONES: I don't see them.

PEER: No. They're not here yet.

MR BONES: On my way here I passed an old man. Said he knew you. Perhaps we should call him.

PEER: He's an old drunk, don't bother.

MR BONES: Well, then, we'd better get on with it—

PEER: Just a minute. Just what are we talking about, here? Be oneself. What the hell does that mean?

MR BONES: You wouldn't understand.

PEER: Try me.

MR BONES: Alright. To be one's self you have to slay one's self.

PEER: Well, that's clear as mud.

MR BONES: You have to give up your vanity, in order to find the Maker within you. You have to still the sound of your own voice, and listen to your true essence. But this is a waste of time, you don't know what I'm talking about—

PEER: Well, you ain't making sense.

MR BONES: Never mind. Come along, now—

PEER: Wait wait wait. I have something to confess. I should've told you this before, but modesty precluded

the full articulation of my multitudinous crimes. I'm really
a very big sinner. A huge sinner. An international sinner.
Abroad, I led the most despicable, dissolute, debauched life
that you can imagine.

MR BONES: Well, if you're that eager to trade the stew pot
for the barbecue pit—

PEER: I prefer it, actually. Must seem kinda extraordinary to
you—

MR BONES: More common that you think. People would
rather be villains than spearcarriers. I want details.

PEER: I'll write you up a full confession.

MR BONES: Well, you'd better hurry. At the next
crossroads—

PEER: I know, I know—

MR BONES: I'll be waiting.

(MR BONES *strolls off.*)

PEER: What I need is a priest. I'll make a full confession,
he'll see I'm beyond absolution, and I'll be saved! Or,
rather, damned!

(PEER *runs off.*)

Scene Eight

(*A hillside of flowers.* PEER *runs on.*)

PEER: Who would have thought that so late in the game, a
shady past would be just the thing to have? It goes to show,
where there's life there's hope, and it ain't over 'til the last
hand's dealt. My lucky day! A priest!

(*A priest enters. It's the* MYSTERIOUS STRANGER *in vestments,
carrying a fishing rod.*)

PEER: A priest gone fishing. Even better. Excuse me, father.

MYSTERIOUS STRANGER: Yes, my son.

PEER: May I speak with you a minute?

MYSTERIOUS STRANGER: Certainly, my boy. Walk with me a
ways.

PEER: Fishing for souls, I see.

MYSTERIOUS STRANGER: As did our Savior, did He not?

PEER: True enough, father, true enough. I've got something on my mind—

MYSTERIOUS STRANGER: Spit it out, son. Make a clean breast of it. You'll feel ever so much better—

PEER: That sounds familiar, somehow. Indeed, there's something about you—well, never mind. Anyway, there are temptations in this world—

MYSTERIOUS STRANGER: Don't I know it!

PEER: And every once in a while, a fellow can't help, well, tasting a forbidden fruit or two—

MYSTERIOUS STRANGER: It's only human—

PEER: Not to say I've done anything truly wicked.

MYSTERIOUS STRANGER: No? Nothing truly wicked? Awful? Evil? Nothing?

PEER: Nah. Penny ante stuff, really, in the great scheme of things. Misdemeanors. Minor transgressions.

MYSTERIOUS STRANGER: Then why are you wasting my time?

PEER: Father?

MYSTERIOUS STRANGER: I'm interested in big-time sin! Monstrous evil! That's what I'm fishing for. Not trivial transgressions! Who cares! How boring!

PEER: Don't you even want to hear what they were?

MYSTERIOUS STRANGER: What do you take me for, the village priest?

PEER: Well, yes, as a matter of fact.

MYSTERIOUS STRANGER: Look closer. See my nails?

PEER: Very long. Very thick. Very strange. Like horn.

MYSTERIOUS STRANGER: What about my foot? The right one.

PEER: Oh, my God. It's. You're. Oh, dear.

MYSTERIOUS STRANGER: Yes. It's me.

PEER: Is that a real hoof?

MYSTERIOUS STRANGER: I like to think so.

PEER: Well, even better. In business, I say, don't bother with the middlemen, the lapdogs, the lackeys, and asslickers—go straight to the top, whoever's in charge. Put 'er there!

(PEER *offers his hand. They shake.*)

MYSTERIOUS STRANGER: Ah. Well. I can see you're an open-minded individual. What can I do for you? If you're looking to sell your soul for money or power, forget it. Times are terrible. Business is lousy, the bottom's dropped out of the market. I just can't get souls to save my life. Everybody's destined for the stew pot these days.

PEER: So I've heard. In fact—

MYSTERIOUS STRANGER: You want a place with me. At my, shall we say, hearth.

PEER: Exactly.

MYSTERIOUS STRANGER: Room and board. A warm room—

PEER: Not *too* warm.

MYSTERIOUS STRANGER: Of course.

PEER: And permission to come and go as I please. To return to the scene of the crime, as it were, if things pick up.

MYSTERIOUS STRANGER: I get these sorts of requests everyday. "Save me from the stewpot. Give me a chance to suffer and repent." I'm very sorry, but there's nothing I can do—

PEER: I tell you, I'm just the sort of client you've been looking for. I trafficked in coolies!

MYSTERIOUS STRANGER: Coolies? Who cares?

PEER: I debauched and exploited! I pillaged! I lied, cheated, and stole!

MYSTERIOUS STRANGER: Not nearly good enough. Others with far more blood on their hands and far graver crimes on their consciences have knocked on my doors and failed to gain entrance. Into the pot with you, my friend. You'll be erased from memory, like you never lived. Your existence will have made absolutely no difference to anyone. Adieu.

PEER: Wait, wait, wait. I more or less let a man drown to save my own skin.

MYSTERIOUS STRANGER: Self preservation, the first duty of any animal. And more or less is rather wishy washy, don't you think? Weak. You can't truthfully say you murdered the man, can you?

PEER: No—

MYSTERIOUS STRANGER: Well, there you are. Not good enough. You merely failed to save him. To put yourself in danger. Perfectly understandable. I saw the whole thing with my own eyes. Now, if you'll excuse me, I have a soul to take delivery of.

PEER: Really? And how did this fellow manage that? What sins did he commit to deserve such V I P treatment?

MYSTERIOUS STRANGER: As far as I know, he's just been himself all of his life. And, after all, that's what counts, when all is said and done.

PEER: How did he manage to do that?

MYSTERIOUS STRANGER: Well, there are two ways one can be oneself. Positively or negatively, like a photograph. Either way gets at the essence of the problem. This fellow was negative, and very much himself, from beginning to end. He was true to his nasty nature, every day of his life. Now, if you'll excuse me.

(*The* MYSTERIOUS STRANGER *tips his hat and goes, leaving* PEER *alone.*)

Scene Nine

(PEER *sits on the hillside. Night falls. A shooting star shoots across the night sky.* PEER *salutes it.*)

PEER: That's a life. Just like that. Flare, and flame, and fade. And disappear. Without a trace. Sad. The soul blazes briefly and then burns itself out. And all that's left is a little ash. Which the wind carries away. The sky is so lovely. The stars. I've never noticed before. I've been preoccupied. All that starlight wasted on me, I suppose. Wasted on my mother, too, for all she made was me, and look how far I've come. Nature is very generous. We don't deserve it.

(MR BONES *appears behind him.*)

MR BONES: Good evening, Mr Gynt. Do you have your confession written up for my perusal?

PEER: No. I racked my brains, but—

MR BONES: Nothing at all?

PEER: Not really. Not worth mentioning.

MR BONES: Well, then. Perhaps it's time—

PEER: No, no, wait—

MR BONES: You're stubborn, I'll give you that—

PEER: Wait! Do you hear that singing?

(The sound of SALLY, *singing in the distance)*

MR BONES: There's an old woman, down the dell—

PEER: There's my sin. There's my crime. Your stew pot's not nearly big enough to hold what I've done to her—

MR BONES: I'll see you at the third crossroads. Third and last—

(He disappears. PEER *follows the sound of* SALLY's *voice.)*

Scene Ten

(The house in the trees. She can be heard singing within. PEER *approaches, hesitantly.)*

PEER: What was it Sasquatch said? Sometimes you have to go the long way 'round? Here I am, finally. At last.

(He stops as SALLY *emerges. She's gone white-haired and blind, but she's still sturdy and serene.)*

PEER: Sally, dear.

SALLY: Who is it?

PEER: I've come back.

SALLY: Peer? Is it really you?

(She goes to him and touches his face.)

PEER: It is me, and I hope you'll speak your piece. Tell me how, and in what ways, I've sinned against you. If you'd care to catalogue my crimes against your person, I'd be most grateful. Please don't spare my feelings. I certainly didn't spare yours.

SALLY: My love. You haven't sinned against me.

PEER: But I have.

(MR BONES *appears in a light.*)

MR BONES: I'm waiting, Peer.

PEER: Call me out, Sally. Tell the world what I did to you.

SALLY: You gave me a great gift.

PEER: Oh, dear. I'm lost. Sally, what are you saying?

SALLY: You made my life into a song. I made a promise to you and I kept it. What could be better than that?

MR BONES: I'm sorry, Peer. If she doesn't bear a grudge, there's nothing I can do—

PEER: Wait! I have one last chance to prove what I've done to her. *(To* SALLY*)* Answer me this, Sally. Where have I been? All these years!

SALLY: Where have you been?

PEER: Yes! All these years! Since I left you! Waiting! I promised to return and never did! Where has Peer Gynt been?

SALLY: Oh, that's easy. Silly boy.

PEER: Is it? Where has Peer Gynt been? Since he's been gone? His true and only self?

SALLY: Here. In my heart. In my faith and love. Here. With me.

(PEER *sinks to his knees, throws his arms around her.*)

PEER: Oh. Oh. My love. Hide me. Hide me in your love.

MR BONES: Peer, my friend. You're reprieved, for now. I'll be waiting for you at the final crossroads. Alki. By and by—

(MR BONES *disappears.* SALLY *strokes* PEER's *head.*)

SALLY: Shh, shh, don't fret, my love. Sleep and dream. I'll protect you. My one and only love. Sweet dreams.

(Lights fade)

END OF PLAY

BROADWAY PLAY PUBLISHING INC
TOP TEN BEST SELLERS
(IN ORDER)

THE COLORED MUSEUM

PRELUDE TO A KISS

ON THE VERGE

TO GILLIAN ON HER 37TH BIRTHDAY

PLAYS BY TONY KUSHNER

TALES OF THE LOST FORMICANS

BEIRUT

DARK RAPTURE

FACING FORWARD

ORGASMO ADULTO ESCAPES FROM THE ZOO

BROADWAY PLAY PUBLISHING INC
ONE ACT COLLECTIONS

BIG TIME & AFTER SCHOOL SPECIAL

ENSEMBLE STUDIO THEATER MARATHON `84

FACING FORWARD

ONE ACTS AND MONOLOGUES FOR WOMEN

ORCHARDS

ORGASMO ADULTO ESCAPES FROM THE ZOO

PLAYS BY LOUIS PHILLIPS

ROOTS IN WATER

SHORT PIECES FROM THE NEW DRAMATISTS

WHAT A MAN WEIGHS &
THE WORLD AT ABSOLUTE ZERO